WE'RE ALONE

ALSO BY EDWIDGE DANTICAT

Fiction

Everything Inside

Claire of the Sea Light

The Dew Breaker

The Farming of Bones

Krik? Krak!

Breath, Eyes, Memory

Nonfiction

The Art of Death: Writing the Final Story

Create Dangerously: The Immigrant Artist at Work

Brother, I'm Dying

After the Dance: A Walk through Carnival in Jacmel, Haiti

Children and Young Adult

My Mommy Medicine

Mama's Nightingale: A Story of Immigration and Separation

Untwine

The Last Mapou

Anacaona, Golden Flower

Eight Days: A Story of Haiti

Behind the Mountains

As Editor

Haiti Noir

Haiti Noir 2: The Classics

Best American Essays 2011

The Butterfly's Way: Voices from the Haitian Dyaspora in the United States

The Beacon Best of 2000: Great Writing by Women and Men of All Colors and Cultures

WE'RE ALONE

ESSAYS

Edwidge Danticat

Graywolf Press

Published by Graywolf Press
212 Third Avenue North, Suite 485
Minneapolis, Minnesota 55401

www.graywolfpress.org

Published in the United States of America
Printed in Canada

ISBN 978-1-64445-302-5 (cloth)
ISBN 978-1-64445-303-2 (ebook)

2 4 6 8 9 7 5 3 1
First Graywolf Printing, 2024

Library of Congress Cataloging-in-Publication Data

Names: Danticat, Edwidge, 1969– author.
Title: We're alone : essays / Edwidge Danticat.
Other titles: We are alone
Description: Minneapolis, Minnesota : Graywolf Press, 2024. | Includes
    bibliographical references.
Identifiers: LCCN 2024004162 (print) | LCCN 2024004163 (ebook) |
    ISBN 9781644453025 (hardcover) | ISBN 9781644453032 (epub)
Subjects: LCGFT: Essays.
Classification: LCC PS3554.A5815 W47 2024 (print) | LCC PS3554.A5815
    (ebook) | DDC 814/.54—dc23/eng/20240126
LC record available at https://lccn.loc.gov/2024004162
LC ebook record available at https://lccn.loc.gov/2024004163

Jacket design: Jeenee Lee

Jacket photo: Widline Cadet, *Seremoni Disparisyon #1
(Ritual [Dis]Appearance #1)*, 2019

Pou Patricia

Contents

We're Alone: A Preface

Your hands—give them to me,
Let me speak, and simply
Words you can not forget. . . .
We're alone—
And the sea . . . .
And the cradling palms are thick.

Roland Chassagne, "Shore"

I spent many years trying to find the original French poem "Plage," from which these lines were translated. I came across the English translation in a 1934 book given to me in the 1990s by a friend. The book is *The Poets of Haiti: 1782–1934*, and the translator is an American writer named Edna Worthley Underwood. Underwood was born in Maine in 1873. I don't know how she ended up in Haiti during the latter end of the 1915–1934 US occupation, but she had friends in high places, including Haitian president Sténio Vincent, who wrote her book's introduction.

Readers will find in *The Poets of Haiti* "the echo of all great human emotions," Vincent declared.

Some of the poems in the collection felt intimate, particularly those by the Jérémie-born poet Roland Chassagne, whose words read like secrets. *We're alone* is the persistent chorus of the deserted, as in *no one is coming to save us*. Yet, *we're alone* can also be a promise writers make to their readers, a reminder of this singular intimacy between us. At least we're alone *together*. Or as A. S. Byatt wrote in her 1990 novel *Possession*, "The writer wrote alone, and the reader read alone, and they were alone with each other."

Writing for me, particularly writing essays, is a quest for that kind of aloneness/togetherness, as well as something akin to what the Haitian American anthropologist and artist Gina Athena Ulysse has labeled *Rasanblaj*, which she defines as "assembly, compilation, enlisting, regrouping (of people, spirits, things, ideas)."

After trying to locate the original Chassagne poem on my own, it finally occurred to me to reach out to Régine Chassagne, a Haitian Canadian musician and one of the lead singers of the indie rock group Arcade Fire. Roland Chassagne was her grandfather. Régine's father, Stanley, sent her a screenshot of the poem, which she shared with me. (See the appendix.) "Plage" was published in a 1933 collection by Roland Chassagne called *Le tambourin voilé* (The Veiled Tambourine). I might have translated the verse differently, if perhaps less lyrically.

Laisse-moi prendre tes mains
Et te dire des choses simples
Et inoubliables . .

Parce que nous étions seuls,
Près du rivage, sous ce dais
des palmes, et qu'on s'aimait,
Le bonheur était intense et
Inexprimable.

Allow me to take you by the hand
And tell you some simple
And unforgettable things . . .

Because we were alone,
Near the shore, under this canopy
Of palms, and we loved each other,
The pleasure was intense and
Indescribable.

In April 1963, during the Duvalier dictatorship, Roland Chassagne was arrested at Port-au-Prince's Deschamps printing house, where he worked as a proofreader. He was accused of being in possession of "contraband literature." Roland Chassagne was taken to François "Papa Doc" Duvalier's prison dungeon, Fort Dimanche, and was never heard from again. His son Stanley, Régine's father, was studying in Chicago at the time and did not hear of the arrest until an aunt traveled there to tell him and other family members. Roland Chassagne was working on an unfinished novel, a copy of which his son Stanley still has. Roland Chassagne's name eventually appeared on a 1978 Inter-American Commission on Human Rights list of political prisoners who had died from malnutrition and disease or had been executed at Fort Dimanche. Still, Roland Chassagne's words remain, both in the original and in somewhat interpretive translations. Writers die, but not their canopy of language. Just as Roland Chassagne still sometimes whispers to me, *Dear Reader, Please allow me to reach for your hand. We're alone.*

WE'RE ALONE

PART 1

Children of the Sea

1

Early in the summer of 2018, I was at the opening of a library in a southern Haitian town called Fond-des-Blancs. Fond-des-Blancs, which means Fountain of Whites, is home to a large number of people of Polish lineage, the descendants of soldiers from a regiment that switched alliances from the French armies they were fighting alongside in early nineteenth-century Haiti to join the Haitians in their battle for independence from France. The mutinous Polish soldiers who settled in Fond-des-Blancs were the only whites and foreigners granted Haitian citizenship after Haiti became the world's first Black republic in 1804.

The library we were there to celebrate had been started by a nonprofit organization called Haiti Projects, which was run by an acquaintance of mine. The opening-week program included writing workshops and conversations with writers. I participated in a conversation and writing workshop with the Haitian novelist and short story writer Kettly Mars. Our moderator, the Haitian educator Jean-Marie Théodat, asked us to read both the beginning and the end of one of our short stories, Kettly in the original French and me in a Haitian Creole translation. We were then asked to explain to the group of twenty-five or so eager teenagers why we'd begun and ended that story the way we had.

It is much easier to explain or elaborate on endings than on beginnings. For endings, you can always say that it ended *this* way because it had begun *that* way. Or it ended that way because something popped up in the middle that led there. Beginnings have more amorphous origins.

I thought of the opening line in an essay by the short story writer and novelist Ann Beattie: "A guilty truth about writing: if you know your subject well, you will never feel assured about where to begin; only boring subjects offer an inevitable starting point."

One of my earliest childhood memories is being torn away from my mother at four. At the airport in Port-au-Prince, on the day my mother left Haiti for the United States, I wrapped my arms around her legs before she headed for the plane. She leaned down and tearfully unballed my fists so my uncle could peel me off her. As my two-year-old brother, André, dropped to the floor, bawling, my mother hurried away, her tear-soaked face buried in her hands. She couldn't bear to look back.

If my life were the short story whose beginning I was asked to explain in that Fond-des-Blancs writing workshop, this might have been my chosen beginning, the most dramatic one I can remember, and which I have spoken of and written about often, including in my memoir *Brother, I'm Dying*. In Haitian Creole, when someone is said to be *lòt bò dlo* on the other side of the water, it can mean either they've traveled abroad or they have died. Even before I knew what it meant, my parents were already *lòt bò dlo*, my father having left for New York two years before my mother. My desire to make sense of this separation, this *lòt bò dlo*-ness, helped me understand that words could bridge distances.

One way I used to communicate with my parents was through letters. Every month my father would send us a brief letter that would begin with "J'écris, espérant que cette missive vous trouve en bonne santé. Moi aussi, je vais bien. Grâce à Dieu." I write, hoping this letter finds you in good health. I, too, am fine. Thanks be to God.

Each time my parents' letters arrived at my uncle's house in Port-au-Prince, I was reminded that my parents could tell me stories from afar. I imagined them telling me cautionary tales, which my uncle often repeated, of my undocumented parents' long, arduous days toiling in sweatshops or about how the immigration police might raid their workplace at any time and take them to a detention center to await deportation. At the workshop in Fond-des-Blancs, the young writers, like so many other young writers elsewhere, kept asking, "How do you begin? Who taught you to write? What do you read? Who do you keep reading?"

My best writing teachers were the storytellers of my childhood, I told them. Most never went to school and never learned to read and write, but they carried stories like treasures inside of them. In my mother's absence, my aunts and grandmothers told me stories in the evenings when the lights went out during blackouts, while they were doing my hair, or while I was doing their hair. This is another possible beginning: stories told to me by women like the ones the late Paule Marshall called "kitchen poets."

2

I moved to New York in 1981 at age twelve to join my parents soon after cases of acquired immunodeficiency syndrome (AIDS) were first discovered in the United States. The Centers for Disease Control named four groups at "high risk" for the disease: intravenous drug users, homosexuals, hemophiliacs, and Haitians. Haitians were the only ones solely identified by nationality, in part because of twenty or so Haitian patients who'd shown up at Jackson Memorial Hospital in Miami. Suddenly, every Haitian was suspected of having AIDS. At the public junior high school where my parents enrolled me, some of the non-Haitian students would regularly shove and hit me and the other Haitian kids, telling us that we had dirty blood. My English as a second language class was excluded from a school trip to the Statue of Liberty out of fear that our sharing a school bus with the other kids might prove dangerous to them.

I had a wonderful teacher at this junior high school, a Haitian exile named Raymond Dusseck. Mr. Dusseck's science, math, and English as a second language lessons relied on games and songs to help us begin speaking in our new tongue. He taught us English songs that were full of stories, starting with the African American national anthem. I remember being enchanted by James Weldon Johnson's beautiful lyrics:

> *Lift every voice and sing,*
> *'Til earth and heaven ring,*
> *Ring with the harmonies of Liberty.*

Eight months later, I was "mainstreamed" from English as a second language to a regular class, where my teacher asked me to write an essay about my first Thanksgiving. I wrote that I was looking forward to eating the "golden" turkey, which I thought was original. Later I would be horrified by my cliché, but she told me I had a great writing voice. *Lift every voice, indeed.* Though not that of the massacred Native Americans.

When I was in the eleventh grade, Mr. Casey, my history teacher at Brooklyn's Clara Barton High School, asked me how I wanted to leave my mark on the world. I told him I wanted to be a writer. The next day, he loaned me his copy of Mari Evans's anthology *Black Women Writers (1950–1980): A Critical Evaluation*. The book included scholarly writings on the works of Paule Marshall, Toni Morrison, Lucille Clifton, Alice Walker, Toni Cade Bambara, Audre Lorde, Gayl Jones, Gwendolyn Brooks, Sonia Sanchez, Nikki Giovanni, Maya Angelou, Gloria Naylor, and many other writers, who would become some of the literary loves of my life. They, along with the Haitian writers I began reading in New York, writers like Marie Vieux-Chauvet, Jacques Roumain, Jacques Stephen Alexis, J. J. Dominique, Ida Faubert, and Dany Laferrière, became my companions on my nascent journey as a writer. (I write about some of these writers elsewhere, including in my 2010 essay collection *Create Dangerously*, which was inspired by Albert Camus and adapted from my lecture in Princeton University's Toni Morrison Lecture Series in March 2008.)

"Can writing change anything?" was another question I was asked at the youth workshop in Fond-des-Blancs. "How does the artist move the world?"

I'm not sure I did, but I wanted to say by bearing witness.

In a 1984 *New York Times* interview, the writer Julius Lester asked the novelist, essayist, and activist James Baldwin: "*Witness* is a word I've heard you use often to describe yourself. . . . What are you witness to?"

Baldwin replied, "Witness to whence I came, where I am. Witness to what I've seen and the possibilities that I think I see."

Though I might not always succeed, this is the kind of writer I would like to be, a witnessing writer.

A friend who was with us in Fond-des-Blancs that day told me that I should write more about love. I considered all I could possibly have to say about love. I told my friend that every word I put down on paper is an act of both witness and love. I thought about what James Baldwin has written about love: *Love does not begin and end the way we seem to think it does. Love is a battle, love is a war; love is a growing up.*

3

In *Dust Tracks on a Road*, the writer and anthropologist Zora Neale Hurston writes that after her mother, Lucy, died, and she left home to travel to places previously unknown to her, she was forced into "the morning of the day of the beginning of things" and that "all that geography was within me. It only needed time to reveal it."

I love this last line so much that sometimes I misquote or paraphrase it as *All geography is within me. It only needs to reveal itself.*

When, after graduating from high school in Brooklyn, I became a student at Zora Neale Hurston's alma mater, Barnard College, I felt as though Zora's ghost was shadowing me. Zora had gone to Haiti to study zombies, Vodou, and folktales. She wrote her most famous novel, *Their Eyes Were Watching God*, there. While Zora's overemphasis on Haitians' "unconscious cruelty," in contrast to her casual dismissal of the brutality of the 1915–1934 US occupation of Haiti and the 1937 massacre of Haitians and Black Dominicans ordered by the Dominican dictator Rafael Trujillo, is agonizing to read in *Tell My Horse*, her chronicles from Haiti still offer the astute perspective of a Black woman anthropologist and creative writer exploring the country's primary religion, Vodou, which continues to be stigmatized and caricatured in the United States.

According to Haitian folklore, eating salt can liberate zombies from their living death. People who suddenly receive terrible news are also given salt, in coffee, for example, to help ward off the *sezisman*, the shock, so that we can pick ourselves up and keep moving. I told the young writers I am a writer because, somehow, I was given the salt. For some of us, that salt is stories and words. For others, it is music, movement, and dance. For others, it is images, shapes, sculpture.

When I first moved to the United States, I remember being shocked that salt was white. In markets in Haiti, we often bought rock sea salt that looked like little crystals or small pebbles, which were unevenly shaped, and had dark streaks either on the surface or inside. You always had to wash the salt pebbles before putting them in food, and even after you washed them, they looked more gray than white.

"The sea is salt," Zora Neale Hurston wrote.

"The sea is history," wrote the Saint Lucian poet Derek Walcott.

In his hybrid poetry and prose collection *Un arc-en-ciel pour l'Occident Chrétien*, translated by the scholar Colin Dayan as *A Rainbow for the Christian West*, the Haitian poet and novelist René Depestre writes that one day water will carry us to the other side of humanity. "Je dis bonjour à cette eau qui nous vient des confins de la douleur! Disons tous bonjour à cette eau qui nous vient des profondeurs de la mer!" (My translation—*I greet this water that comes to us from the depths of pain! Let us all greet this water that comes to us from the depths of the sea!*)

The story whose beginning I chose to explain to the teenagers at the library in Fond-des-Blancs is from my 1995 short story collection *Krik? Krak!* and is called "Children of the Sea." It's about a group of Haitian refugees trying to reach the United States by boat after a US-supported 1991 military coup d'état against Haiti's first democratically elected president, Jean-Bertrand Aristide.

I began the story the way I did, I told them—with the lines

"They say behind the mountains are more mountains. Now I know it's true."—because it evokes a Haitian proverb I love—*dèyè mòn gen mòn*. I also told them that writing that story, and all my stories, reaffirms my belief that being human means having to keep beginning again.

4

After we left Fond-des-Blancs, my husband and I and our two daughters went to spend two weeks with my mother-in-law in Gros Marin, a small rural village further south. Our US-born niece, who was in Haiti for the first time, joined us there. Suddenly a whole new generation of our family, from the millennials to the preteens, wanted to visit Haiti. They were telling us that they didn't want to visit "Resort Haiti"—which we were not that familiar with anyway—but wanted to see what they were calling "the Real Haiti," or as real as we, their diaspora relatives, could show them.

My eighty-six-year-old mother-in-law, who, when she was in the countryside, chose to live, for the most part, the same way her grandparents had, could always be counted on to provide a rustic experience. One of the three bungalows on her property—the one my husband, daughters, and I usually slept in—had a thatch roof. Behind our bedroom was a much smaller room where we showered using plastic buckets filled with water we pumped ourselves from her well. For a more luxurious bath, we could walk down to the river, which our niece did in the most elaborate white ruffled two-piece bathing suit that anyone in my mother-in-law's village (and probably on most American beaches) had ever seen. At night we peed in chamber pots if we were too scared to walk out to the latrine in the dark. The foods we ate were mostly from my mother-in-law's garden or had been traded for other foods from her neighbors' gardens. When we were served chicken, it was likely that we had met the bird earlier in the day, which led to my husband, who'd spent his childhood summers in the same area, being the only one in our group eating those meals in their entirety. Our niece took all of this in the way young people process experiences, with her smartphone. She texted, Snapchatted, Instagrammed, and Facebooked everything to her hundreds of social media followers.

We did our best to stay one step ahead of the heat. There was the river, which was crowded with local bathers every afternoon. We also drove out to the beach but could not go in the water. Most of the beaches on the southern coast were covered in red tide, toxic algae that made them look as though millions of dead brown leaves were either bobbing on the waves or had washed ashore. The combination of the algae and the human-produced waste—plastic and foam containers being the most prevalent—made swimming impossible.

After our niece returned to Miami, we devoted ourselves entirely to watching World Cup games in the backyard of a neighbor who happened to have a television and was charging people the equivalent of a quarter to watch each game. The World Cup was an obsession in our area, as it was in the rest of Haiti, where the Brazilian team is a perennial favorite. There were Brazilian flags everywhere—on cars, motorcycles, and homes—not because Brazil had led MINUSTAH, a multibillion-dollar, decade-long United Nations peacekeeping debacle in Haiti from 2004 to 2017, or because thousands of Haitians had migrated to Brazil after the January 12, 2010, earthquake, but because most Haitians, like many other soccer fans around the world, claim Brazil's team as their own. They hoped the Brazilian team would win its sixth World Cup in the last sixty years.

One sweltering early July day, we drove to the home of a family friend in Port Salut, a beautiful coastal town about thirty miles from my mother-in-law's house, to watch Brazil face Belgium in the quarterfinals. So many of our friend's neighbors had come to watch the game that he pitched a makeshift tent in front of his house to accommodate us all. When the match ended, and Brazil lost, scoring only one goal to Belgium's two, the young woman sitting next to me began sobbing. I thought she was a superfan who was overcome with grief at the loss, but as she rocked herself, she said, "What am I going to do with all the machandiz?"

She'd been hoping that the Brazilian team would make it to the finals, she said, and had gotten a high-interest loan to buy Brazil-related merchandise—jerseys, flags, and bracelets—to sell. Now the items had plunged in value, and she was deep in debt. Her anguish was a heartrending reminder that the fate of some of the most disadvantaged people in the world is linked to factors far beyond their control.

Port Salut felt like a graveyard when we left it that evening, not just because of the disappointment over the World Cup. During Brazil's final match, the Haitian government, led by President Jovenel Moïse and Prime Minister Jack Guy Lafontant, had announced that to ensure the country would qualify for low-interest loans from the International Monetary Fund, they were raising the price of gasoline and diesel. As a result, the cost of kerosene, which was used to light most homes in the Haitian countryside, increased by 51 percent. We only heard the news on the drive back to my mother-in-law's when we began receiving messages from family members and friends advising us to get off the road. We encountered nearly a dozen roadblocks on the way, most of them made from piles of rocks and flaming tires guarded by anxious young men, some of them waving handguns. After fleeing one where a man was shooting in the air, we retreated to a dry riverbed where we encountered a young mototaxi driver, who, while explaining why he and his friends would not let us through, detailed how the sudden gas hike would chip away at the life they were struggling to build for themselves and their families.

"We want a future, but they keep snatching it away," he said.

When we finally made it back to my mother-in-law's house, we waited a few days until the demonstrations quieted down before leaving for Port-au-Prince to catch our scheduled flight to Miami. We left late one afternoon, and as we departed the countryside, it began to rain. The roads were mostly deserted, in part because of the rain but also because of the recent protests. We came across remnants of several roadblocks along the way: half-melted tires, blackened river rocks, fallen palm trees, around which our friend and Tour Haiti driver, Solage, carefully skirted his pickup truck.

We were relieved as we approached Port-au-Prince since we thought we were leaving behind, in the countryside, the greater possibility of overflowing rivers and mudslides strong enough to overtake Solage's jeep in the rain. As we approached the city's outskirts, I saw what seemed like a shimmery river extending for miles and miles. Solage was uncertain about how to proceed. It was hard to tell how deep the water was or where the car might sink or get stuck. Solage moved carefully, staying close to the front porches of houses and patches of sidewalk that were still visible.

As the car made its way through the tightly packed surface of this street river, the water parted, and on either side of us were hundreds of plastic water and soda bottles mixed with foam boxes, which in the limited light seemed to glow. During heavy rains in Port-au-Prince, a large number of people—with no sanitation system to speak of and no regular pickup—throw their trash in the surge of water suddenly gushing in front of their homes. We did this in the house I lived in as a child, not thinking where this trash would end up. Our trash probably resurfaced in a place like this, in a stream of rubbish seeking a path to the ocean.

Our trash was mainly fruit and vegetable husks and peels. We reused everything else. The Carnation milk cans became lamps (*tèt gridap*), and occasional glass jars or plastic bottles were used to store castor, cooking oil, or kerosene. Now so much of the trash is plastic or Styrofoam that it floats by the tons on top of flowing or agitated waters, reminding me of images I have seen of vortexes and plastispheres in both the Atlantic and the Pacific Oceans, most famously the Great Pacific Garbage Patch that stretches between California and Hawaii.

A few weeks after we found ourselves in this river of debris, Hurricane Florence struck North Carolina, and debris from Haiti and the Dominican Republic, including shampoo, vinegar, and ketchup bottles, and relaxer containers with Spanish and Creole labeling, washed up on much-frequented North Carolina beaches.

"I can't fathom the volume of trash that must be floating in the ocean from that one small island. It is a serious problem when a shoreline over 1,100 miles away is tainted," a Charlotte resident told his local newspaper.

Our small island did not invent this trash. Ironically, a flatbed truck from the Dominican Republic was stuck in the trash river with us. The truck was carrying hundreds of bottles filled with fluorescent juices and sodas heading to market: for schoolchildren to put in lunch boxes, to be enjoyed at parties, or during days spent at beaches, some of which are covered with bottles like these. Even if all the plastic in the water that night was instantly removed and recycled, those bottles on the truck were waiting to replace it. Not to mention the foam food boxes, single-use bags, and discarded used clothes (*pèpè*) shipped in bales to Haiti daily.

It feels theatrical to admit, but while the car was wading through that river of foam and plastic, and God knows what else, with Solage and my husband and daughters watching, I felt like screaming, "The land might never be pristine again." This land of mountains beyond mountains has already seen genocide after Christopher Columbus and the Spaniards arrived in 1492 and either killed outright or worked the Taíno and Arawak to death for their gold. This land where enslaved Africans were then brought to be brutalized by the Spanish, British, and French until the enslaved people and some free men and women, and some mutinous Polish soldiers whose descendants now live in Fond-des-Blancs, battled for independence and created the world's first Black republic. This land was forced to spend the first century of its existence paying $150 million (now worth close to $30 billion) indemnity to France for this independence. Americans invaded and then occupied this land for nineteen years at the beginning of the twentieth century. This land endured the murderous thirty-year dictatorial Duvalier dynasty until 1986. This land elected its first democratically elected president, Jean-Bertrand Aristide, in 1990 only to have him overthrown in a coup d'état carried out by the Haitian military—some of whose members had been trained in the United States and were on the CIA's payroll—and deposed again in 2004 after his reelection. This land was devastated by a massive earthquake that killed over two hundred thousand people in 2010. This land was struck by several destructive hurricanes soon after. This land where United Nations "peacekeepers" introduced a cholera epidemic that has killed over ten thousand people and has affected close to a million, increasing the use of water bottles as carriers for "safe" or filtered water. This land where, at the same time that we saw this river of scraps and discards, protesters were demanding the ouster of their president over fuel price hikes and corruption, most recently embezzled funds from Petrocaribe, an oil alliance between Venezuela and some Caribbean states, including Haiti.

In the Caribbean tourism market, the "hot" places quickly clean up their trash. However, those who can't afford to clean up a river or rain drain full of plastic and foam in the middle of a city will have to live with their trash. Or they might burn the garbage themselves. And burning one's own garbage, as many do in Haiti—from those living in the middle of the city to those residing in the most remote rural areas—now means using fire to break down plastic and foam polymers. This trash is not just migrating from land mass to oceans and back. It is also migrating into our blood, lungs, placentas, breast milk, and our brains.

Three decades earlier, in 1988, a garbage barge named the *Khian Sea* dropped four thousand tons of incinerated trash ash from Philadelphia on the shores of Gonaïves, a historic northern Haitian city and one of the country's largest. The *Khian Sea* had been sailing worldwide for years, looking for a place to unload its cargo in the Bahamas, the Dominican Republic, Bermuda, Panama, Honduras, then Senegal, Cape Verde, Guinea-Bissau, Sri Lanka, Indonesia, Borneo, and the Philippines. The barge was turned away from these ports. Then a group of Haitian politicians accepted bribes in exchange for having a portion of the *Khian Sea*'s fourteen thousand–ton cargo, which was labeled as fertilizer, discarded on a beach in Haiti. (The rest was dumped in the Atlantic and Indian Oceans.) The ash, in the care of a waste disposal company hired by the city of Philadelphia, was later found to contain lead, chromium, and dioxin, a toxic environmental pollutant and a known carcinogen.

I can't help but think of the trash that ended up on the beaches of North Carolina during Hurricane Florence, in the summer of 2018, as a kind of revenge. The *Khian Sea* ash spent twelve years on the beach in Gonaïves before the Haitian government, with help from the environmental organization Greenpeace, pressured the waste disposal company to take what was left of the ash to a landfill in Philadelphia, just a few miles from where it began its decade-plus journey.

There's a Haitian proverb that says *Lanmè pa kenbe kras*. The sea does not hold dirt. This saying might have come down to us from the combined knowledge of our indigenous ancestors, who ate from the sea their whole lives, and our African ancestors, so many of whom were brutally transported across the ocean on slave ships. The sea welcomed the bodies of those who jumped off those ships and never made it across—cleansing them. (It does not hold dirt, thus we are not dirt.) Our ancestors might have also been speaking of a cleaner, more pristine sea.

Illustrating that some creatures will overcome impossible odds to survive, in early 2023, scientists from the journal *Nature Ecology and Evolution* found close to five hundred invertebrate species growing on the soupy plastic debris of the Great Pacific Garbage Patch, over a thousand miles from the nearest land. The invertebrates detected in the Great Pacific Garbage Patch trash vortex—anemones, barnacles, hydroids, mussels, oysters, sponges, and worms—usually make their home along coastlines and were thought to be incapable of surviving in open seas. Pushed by wind and currents, they have migrated just as humans have been forced or chosen to do since the beginning of time. These coastal creatures have adapted to their new circumstances while coming into contact with open-sea creatures they might have never encountered before. The ocean is not their final destination. They might travel further still, the scientists believe, and become invasive species on newer (to them) shores.

"As humans, we are creating new types of ecosystems that have potentially never been seen before," a biogeographer told the *Atlantic* magazine in 2023. In other words, we are creating potentially beautiful, or potentially tragic, new beginnings.

We are the children of these seas as well.

A Rainbow in the Sky

It's hard to describe to people who have never experienced a major hurricane what it's like to live through one. The pounding torrential rains. The roaring gale-force winds uprooting and tossing giant trees as though they were twigs. The relentlessness of it all heightens your doubts about your creaking house's ability to remain standing. It is as if the air you are accustomed to breathing has suddenly gathered supernatural force and become angry and decided to try to kill you. Then there's the sudden stillness of the eye, with its clear skies and its deceptively light, sometimes even warm, breezes, followed by the brutal force on the back end of the storm, reminding you that there's still a catastrophic doughnut rotating in the sky.

The less stable your house, the more terror you feel. I remember my parents describing their fright as they trembled inside their respective homes—my mother's a wooden tin-covered house, my father's a concrete one—while Hurricane Flora, a Category 4 storm, roared through Haiti in October 1963. Ask any Haitian who is old enough to remember, and you might still be able to detect a remnant of alarm. Flora, which also struck Cuba and the Bahamas, was responsible for thousands of deaths in Haiti.

I only remember two hurricanes when I lived in Haiti as a child. Hurricane David made landfall in the northern part of the country, in late August 1979, as a Category 3 storm. David had a high death toll in the neighboring Dominican Republic, where it struck as a Category 5. No deaths were officially attributed to David in Haiti, though my family members were sure many went unnoted—deaths in remote rural regions of the country are rarely accurately reported. The following year, in August of 1980, Hurricane Allen brushed past Haiti's southern coast. It did not make landfall but still took several hundred lives in floods and mudslides. At the time, I was living in Port-au-Prince, whose surrounding mountain ranges offer some buffer and act as a partial shield against hurricane-force winds, even if they don't provide much protection against the pounding rain. Flooding would continue even after the rain had stopped, carrying dozens of people away.

The first hurricanes I experienced in the United States made landfall in Florida during the brutal 2005 season, which brought three Category 5 storms, most famously the catastrophic Katrina, in August. My daughter Mira was five months old when Katrina struck New Orleans and the Mississippi Gulf Coast. I held Mira tightly as my husband and I spent hours watching the bloated cadavers of men and women floating down the inundated streets of New Orleans on our television screen. In addition to sorrow and horror, we felt a kinship with the survivors, who, like us, had been born and raised in the paths of such storms and were now living in their crosshairs in Miami.

In October 2016, Haiti found itself in the crosshairs of Hurricane Matthew. A Category 4 storm with 145-mile-per-hour winds, Matthew made landfall in the southwest region of the country, decimating large portions of it. Towns were nearly annihilated, with most houses either roofless or flattened. Farmlands and roads were flooded, and rivers raged, demolishing bridges. Five hundred and forty-six people were reported dead. Cell phones were down for days, making contacting friends and family in the south impossible. It was just as difficult to reach family members after the devastating 7.0 magnitude earthquake killed an estimated two hundred thousand on January 12, 2010. Thoughts of the earthquake brought to mind the dilemma of living in seismic and hurricane-prone areas: concrete might protect you from hurricanes but can become deadly during an earthquake.

Before Matthew made landfall, the last contact I had with my friends in Gros Marin was the day before the hurricane struck, when I asked where they would take shelter. Most of them did not seem worried.

"There will always be storms," one friend said, stressing that the previous one, Hermine, had recently bypassed them altogether.

The night Hurricane Matthew came ashore, I stayed up with my mother-in-law, who was visiting us in Miami. We listened to live Haitian radio reports online. People were calling in from coastal areas to say that the sea was coming into the towns, farms, and churches where they had sought shelter. Some eventually had to leave those shelters in the dark to seek higher ground. The calls to the radio stations were brief and urgent. Before he was abruptly cut off, one man said he heard a group screaming inside a house as the sea lapped at its doors.

My mother-in-law eventually learned, through a text sent by one of her neighbors, that her home had been severely damaged. Like hers, most of her neighbors' houses were either mangled or smashed by winds and floods. We learned that twenty people were sleeping in one room in the large concrete building near my mother-in-law's home. As it traveled over southern Haiti, Hurricane Matthew killed livestock and destroyed crops. There were reports of people having no food, water, or shelter and living in caves while eating potentially toxic plants on the outskirts of Jérémie. The Haitian government estimated the hurricane caused up to $2.9 billion in damages. Also looming was the increased menace of waterborne illnesses, including cholera. The day after the storm, our friend Phillipe sent us a picture of the sky above what was left of my mother-in-law's house. Behind the clouds was a rainbow, and it looked like a sphere, a massive circle.

A few months later, I was standing on the back of a pickup truck to address a hundred or so protesters gathered in front of the Miami field office of the US Citizenship and Immigration Services. We were asking the Department of Homeland Security to prolong temporary protected status, or TPS, for Haitians, who first gained the designation after the January 2010 earthquake, and needed it even more as a result of the hurricane. Temporary protected status—which DHS grants to individuals who cannot return to their home countries because of wars, epidemics, or grave natural disasters—typically lasts eighteen months. However, some countries that have benefited, including Honduras and Nicaragua, have had the status for over twenty years.

I was expressing my support for the extension of TPS for over sixty thousand Haitians when a loud cheer broke out, and everyone started pointing upward at the sky. Out of nowhere, a rainbow ring emerged in the cloudless midmorning sky. It inspired such jubilation that I had to step aside.

I handed the microphone to Farah Juste, a well-known Haitian singer and community activist. She began singing "Alelouya pou Ayiti" (Hallelujah for Haiti), one of her most famous compositions. Juste's robust voice and upbeat lyrics reminded me of Mahalia Jackson singing her heart out in one of my gospel favorites, "God Put a Rainbow in the Sky":

> *God put a rainbow in the sky . . .*
> *It looked like the sun wasn't gon' shine no more*
> *Oh, God put a rainbow in the sky*

Juste was followed by a preacher who reaffirmed what I as-
sumed everyone was thinking: the rainbow was a clear and posi-
tive sign that temporary protected status would be extended for
the next eighteen months. After that, all would be well until the
next renewal date.

I used to think that a circular rainbow was a rare optical illusion until someone told me that most rainbows are circular; we
just can't always see both sides. I had never seen a complete circular rainbow in person before that moment. Rainbows, I was
taught, as the daughter of a Pentecostal deacon and the niece
of a Baptist minister, are meant to remind us of biblical floods,
like the one Noah survived in his ark. Rainbows are also seen, in
many cultures, as bridges between our world and the next. Iris,
the Greek rainbow goddess, is a messenger between gods, mor-
tals, clouds, and the sea. The Haitian rainbow lwa or spirit, Ayida
Wèdo, is also the goddess of water, wind, fire, and serpents. She is
sometimes referred to as the Rainbow Serpent and is believed by
the Fon people of Benin to hold up the sky. In *A Rainbow for the
Christian West*, René Depestre has Simbi, the *lwa* or spirit of rivers, demand the blood of a poet in exchange for a rainbow, even
a rainbow that is beneath the ocean, *un arc-en-coeur*, "a heartbow of the sea," in Colin Dayan's beautiful translation. A friend
at the TPS demonstration told me that in parts of Latin America,
some mothers hide their children from rainbows or instruct them
not to look or point at them because they're manifestations of the
devil's anger.

Our circular rainbow lasted nearly thirty minutes before fading
as the demonstration ended. Nine days later, President Donald J.
Trump's Department of Homeland Security announced that
temporary protected status for Haitians would be extended for only
six more months before more than a hundred thousand people
could potentially be deported. Subsequent extensions were granted

through 2020 by court order after a group of lawyers and activists sued the Trump administration. Then later, the Biden administration extended TPS in May 2021. The rainbow seemed to have been a bearer of good news, even if it was delivered in a prolonged and chaotic fashion.

On Labor Day weekend 2019, Dorian, a Category 5 hurricane, pummeled the Bahamas and pulverized homes on Abaco and Grand Bahama Islands with wind gusts of over two hundred miles an hour. The hurricane hovered for forty-eight hours, crawling between one and three miles per hour. Dorian inundated the islands with three feet of rain, and a storm surge of over twenty feet, leading to dozens of deaths, including that of a still unknown number of Haitians and Bahamians of Haitian descent living on the islands. During the storm, Denis Phillips, a meteorologist from Tampa, Florida, tweeted an image showing a circular rainbow wrapped around Hurricane Dorian's expansive eye. The image was said to be from NASA, but it did not look like the white-and-gray ones usually used by NASA on weather forecasts.

Hurricane Dorian's TV rainbow eye was a kind of coding, a series of radar screen colors designed to identify the intensity levels inside the storm. Blue meant light, green moderate, yellow heavy, red and orange severe, and violet or purple, extreme. The rainbow around Hurricane Dorian's eye went from a light to a darker blue at the immediate center, then green and yellow as it spread out, then bright red and violet on the farther edges.

I once made a rainbow. In a science class in high school, I performed an experiment in which I filled a glass jar with water and put a mirror next to it at a forty-five-degree angle. I aimed the mirror at a dark part of the school lab's wall. And sure enough, there emerged a rainbow. Not a perfectly arced or circular one, but a fat uneven one with pale and unsteady variations of blue, yellow, orange, and green. After seeing the rainbow at the demonstration, I tried to make that same kind of rainbow again at my writing desk and failed. Only the water-filled glass was reflected in the mirror back at me.

Soon after Hurricane Dorian ravaged several islands in the Bahamas, the United Nations' Intergovernmental Panel on Climate Change reminded us that by 2050 oceans will rise high enough to wipe out low-lying cities like Miami. Hurricanes, extreme heat, droughts, floods, and wildfires will displace over a quarter of a billion people. These are enough people to create what could be the fifth-largest country in the world, a migrating nation with no landmass, borders, railways, roadways, seaports, airports, schools, hospitals, communications, financial institutions, or disaster management systems, all of which they'll need to acquire from the other nations that have somehow managed to escape their fate. The unwanted citizens of this pariah state will soon be arriving in even more significant numbers at every remaining border. They will be trafficked, smuggled, crammed by the millions into refugee camps, whipped by immigration officers, shot at by armies, abandoned to freeze in tundra, and die of thirst in deserts. They will continue to drown by the thousands at sea, even as their deaths are recorded and viewed over and over by millions. Few countries will want to embrace or absorb this populace, yet no fences, walls, or armies will hold them back. They will be migrating not to chase dreams or procure luxuries but for food and water. They will be escaping the land, water, and food wars being fought over the little that's left. They will still be called invaders, infiltrators, animals, an ongoing crisis, a national security threat, specters some will say they did not see coming but, like the other half of the rainbow, the heartbow, have been there all along.

"I have become a river," they might each proclaim, just as the Haitian poet and novelist René Depestre has before them, in his poem "La rivière" (The River), as translated by Colin Dayan.

> *There now, it is done, I have become a river.*
> *It will be a great adventure all the way to the sea.*
> *What name will they give me on the maps?*
> *From where does this stream of unknown water come?*
> *What sky does it reflect with its waves?*
> *What calm, what hunger, what sorrow?*

They Are Waiting in the Hills

Traveling with Lorraine Hansberry, Audre Lorde,
James Baldwin, Gabriel García Márquez, Paule Marshall,
and Toni Morrison

Hansberry

I slept through my first big New York City blizzard at sixteen. I woke up to the sound of a shovel grating the sidewalk as our neighbor, Mrs. Clark, cleared a path to her car. Snow was a striking transition from one culture to another, more abrupt than leaves turning in the fall. No one on our block in East Flatbush, Brooklyn, owned a large snowblower and the sanitation trucks took at least a day to arrive, so the snow would stay put for a while, like a thick white blanket over a lumpy bed. Flurries were still streaming past the streetlamp in front of our house when I woke up for school. Daylight had been delayed by snowflakes dancing past the lamp's foggy rays.

Grail was the only thing that impressed me as much as the snow. Some summers, high in the mountains in the Haitian countryside, where I spent my childhood summers, it would suddenly start to rain in the middle of the day, and out of the rain would emerge perfectly round pellets, as solid as roadside pebbles but colder than anything I'd ever felt. Even my brother and cousin, who, at any sign of rain, liked to jump out of our countryside relatives' houses naked for outdoor baths, would stay inside when there was grail because we had been told a fantastical cautionary tale: that each marble-sized orb could get larger and larger until it became a boulder and flattened everything. But as soon as the rain stopped, we'd head out for small piles of grail, stuff them in our mouths, and suck on them as though they were glacial treats from God's refrigerator.

I would always think of grail during New York blizzards, when the snow flew around wildly as though being guided by hurricane-strength winds. In high school, my best friend, Norma, and I would go to the Brooklyn Botanic Garden after a fresh fall in search of the best snow. Mostly a haven for greenhouses, flower cultivation, and weddings, the Brooklyn Botanic Garden was regularly opened for a few hours in the winter. The trees looked like ghosts, miles and miles of leaf-stripped phantoms neatly lined up on either side of both wide and narrow trails. Sometimes Norma and I would attack a whole field with our black rubber boots, leaving behind two lines of footprints while imagining that someone would come back later in the night to track them with search dogs and helicopters. We had just read Jack London's *Call of the Wild* in Mr. Swizohn's tenth-grade English class, and one of my favorite scenes was of the central subject and character, Buck, touching snow for the first time.

> *Buck's feet sank into a white mushy something very like*
> *mud. . . . It bit like fire, and the next instant was gone.*
> *This puzzled him . . . It was his first snow.*

Norma had a crush on Mr. Swizohn, our bearded, redheaded English teacher, who once asked me to make a dinner reservation for him, *en français*, at the French restaurant where he was to propose to his girlfriend. Norma was devastated when I told her about his engagement. Still, she quickly blew it off by laughing at the fact that, being new to English, I was long past the first chapter of *Call of the Wild* before realizing that Buck was a dog and not a man. When Norma was done making fun of me, she swooned over how Mr. Swizohn could recite long passages from *Romeo and Juliet, Othello, King Lear,* and *The Winter's Tale,* passages that we were made to memorize for his class.

"Everyone should commit a little Shakespeare to memory," Mr. Swizohn would say before making us perform scenes like actors at a table read. I hated to be chosen for any part because I had a heavy Haitian Creole accent, which made Shakespeare's convoluted language sound even more incomprehensible to my classmates.

Norma and I would test each other to see if we remembered our soliloquies as we walked in the Botanic Garden in the snow. We would stretch our imaginations to reach for even the most remote connection to our chalky surroundings, reciting to each other Autolycus's boasts of his imported wares in *The Winter's Tale.*

> *Lawn as white as driven snow,*
> *Cyprus black as e'er was crow . . .*

The night before, on television, Norma had seen the film version of Lorraine Hansberry's play *A Raisin in the Sun,* starring Sidney Poitier. We both loved Sidney Poitier and Harry Belafonte, whom we thought of as "island men."

"Why can't we read that play and memorize those lines?" she asked, stomping on a thawing circle of brown dirt near the trail's end.

Norma particularly liked one of the speeches made by the

younger sister in the play, the rebellious Beneatha, and tried to recite some version of it for me with the same emotion that the actress who'd played Beneatha, the vibrant Diana Sands, had.

> *When I was very small . . . we used to take our sleds out in the wintertime and the only hills we had were the ice-covered stone steps of some houses down the street.*

"Those things relate much more to our lives," Norma said, then added breathlessly, as she had many times before, "I'd love to come here with Sidney and not you."

"That's okay," I'd say, "because Harry and I would be in a much warmer place. Haiti, Barbados, Jamaica, or Trinidad."

Even as we discussed our famous paramours, I kept thinking of Lorraine Hansberry because she was a writer, and I, too, wanted to become a writer. Lorraine Hansberry died at thirty-four, and I'd always feared, from the time that I was collecting grail on the top of Haitian mountains, that I might die young. So, as we talked about Lorraine Hansberry, Norma and I walked the rest of the trail in silence, in Lorraine Hansberry's memory, dejectedly pondering the loss of the old woman she would never become.

When I got home, my father, who'd been living with snow longer than we had, told my brothers and me to be careful the next few days. He said the snowflakes would no longer stick to the tall green ash tree growing out of the sidewalk in front of our house. Instead, in a few days, the temperature would spike and then drop, turning clusters of snowflakes into deadly icicles that might pierce our bodies, gliding dangerously from the top of our heads to the soles of our feet.

By dusk, the path Mrs. Clark tried to clear to her car had already disappeared. We had not cleared our driveway, so an even thicker rug of snow lay there. A single moving car, a phone company van, plowed through on its way to salvage fallen lines. Even in the snow, these phone lines seemed to stretch between ourselves and some very distant place, perhaps to Buck, Sidney, Harry, and Lorraine Hansberry, sitting on an ice-covered hill somewhere, writing a few more words for us.

Lorde

I was heading to Grenada while the island was hosting the 2017 State of the Tourism Industry Conference, one of the region's largest gatherings on the subject. Though the conference was planned before Hurricanes Irma and Maria devastated many Caribbean islands whose economies rely heavily on tourism, the timing seemed prescient. Indeed, on the conference program I scrolled through on the plane were discussions focused on disaster preparedness, recovery, and rebuilding. I was not attending the conference, though, because I am not a tourism expert. The people sitting on the plane on either side of me were not tourism experts either. They were tourists, two young American couples on their honeymoons. After listening to them exchange wedding stories, I turned to the poet and essayist Audre Lorde's "Grenada Revisited: An Interim Report," an essay she wrote a few weeks after the 1983 US invasion of her parents' homeland.

I had read Lorde's essay many times before—it's the last chapter of her seminal 1984 collection *Sister Outsider*—but I wanted to reread it before seeing Grenada for the first time. That we landed at Maurice Bishop International Airport, which is named after the former prime minister of Grenada, who was assassinated six days before the start of the US invasion, might have intrigued Lorde. I felt her begin this journey with me as I walked down the airplane steps, the sun that is only this sparkling bright in the Caribbean beaming down on my face.

"The first time I came to Grenada I came seeking 'home,'" began Lorde's essay about her 1978 visit. She had flown into the now-closed Pearl's Airport in Grenville on the island's northeastern coast. Back then, there was one paved road, she reported. Now, there are many smooth and winding ones through lively neighborhoods and tree-covered hills.

Among Lorde's most vivid recollections was seeing Grand Anse Beach, not the hotel-lined miles of white sand that attract both locals and tourists but the busy thoroughfare that runs alongside it. She saw: "Children in proper school uniforms carrying shoes, trying to decide between the lure of a coco palm adventure to one side and the delicious morning sea on the other."

I, too, saw children, dozens of them, on either side of the street one morning. Most wore traditional island school uniforms, white shirts or blouses, with plaid skirts or khakis. They huddled together, chatting and giggling, not paying attention to the dark blue sea on one side or the colorfully painted houses and buildings in the hills on the other. They reminded me of children you would see heading to school in Port-au-Prince, their range of black and brown skin glistening in the sun. The older ones kept their younger siblings at their side, even as they climbed into minivans and buses.

I went in search of more of those "vivid images" Lorde evokes in her essay, and, besides the students at Grand Anse Beach, there was the Fat-Woman-Who-Fries-Fish-in-the-Market. I did not see the Fat-Woman-Who-Fries-Fish-in-the-Market inside the turquoise-and-white square building downtown. She was not standing near the enormous fish on slabs waiting to be gutted. Nor was she by the smaller ones piled into buckets out front. The fish market smelled predictably like the sea. The buzz of the customer and buyer exchanges was much more subdued than I expected. Only some of the vendors had customers. The market's calm on a Friday afternoon reminded me how small Grenada is. The island is 134.6 square miles, home to about a hundred thousand residents.

At dusk, in my ocean-facing hotel room at the Coyaba Beach Resort, I parted the curtains and waited for the sunset to momentarily turn the sand on the beach "flash green," the same kind of faster-than-the-blink-of-an-eye green ray that Paule Marshall had tried to catch every afternoon while she was living in Grenada in 1962. Unfortunately, October is the wrong time of year for this. Audre Lorde had seen her green flash and a full moon in April.

In her memoir *Triangular Road*, Paule Marshall writes that Grenada "suggested the Eden the world had once been."

I was in Grenada to receive an honorary degree from the University of the West Indies Open Campus. The students in the 2017 graduating class hailed from all over the English-speaking Caribbean and earned their degrees online. Many had lost homes and loved ones. I was told the story of one graduate from Trinidad who stayed home because she had donated her plane ticket money to relief efforts in Dominica, which has UWI's most devastated campus. Hurricane Maria had struck Dominica, the southernmost of the Leeward Islands, as a Category 5 storm on September 18. Dominica's prime minister, Roosevelt Skerrit, whose roof collapsed during the storm, later told CNN: "Our agriculture sector is 100 percent destroyed. Our tourism is, I would say, about 95 percent destroyed."

In front of the supermarket across from the Coyaba Beach Resort were blue barrels lined up to collect food and other urgently needed supplies for Dominica. At the Beach House Restaurant, just north of the airport, where I attended a pregraduation cocktail party the night before the ceremony, the young female singer

entertaining us with classic soul as well as Caribbean covers reminded everyone to drop something in the basket that would
usually hold her tips; the funds would go to Dominica.

I have never been to Dominica, but now I wish I had. This
is not born just from a desire to see a place "before." Before the
devastation, before the storm. I am from a place that constantly
evokes nostalgia in the people who have seen, lived, and loved it
"before." This longing for before always saddens me because it
makes the present seem even worse. But I still wish I had seen
Dominica before, partly because it is the birthplace of the novelist
Jean Rhys. I wish I had seen all that Antoinette, Rhys's doomed
narrator in *Wide Sargasso Sea*, had longed for from her captivity
in Mr. Rochester's England: flaming sunsets and rivers so clear
that you can see the pebbles at the bottom, the moss-covered gardens filled with orchids, hibiscus, and flamboyants, which are
illuminated at night by fireflies.

This is one of the ways I have imagined Dominica, along with
what I have seen in travel guides: its high mountain peaks, forts,
lush rainforests, reefs, gorges, lakes, and waterfalls. Dominica is
also home to Xuela Claudette Richardson, the narrator of Jamaica
Kincaid's novel *The Autobiography of My Mother*. At fifteen, Xuela
is taken by her father to Roseau, the capital of Dominica. Roseau,
Xuela finds, has—like many places in the Caribbean—"a fragile
foundation, and from time to time was destroyed by forces of
nature, a hurricane or water coming from the sky as if suddenly
the sea were above and the heavens below."

"The second time I came to Grenada," Audre Lorde wrote in
"Grenada Revisited," "I came in mourning and fear that this land
which I was learning had been savaged, invaded, its people ma-
neuvered into saying thank you to their invaders."

Lorde's second visit was in late 1983 after US president Ronald
Reagan had deployed marines to the island. Reagan declared

that he wanted to prevent a "Soviet-Cuban" colony from taking root in Grenada and protect American citizens on the island, many of whom were students at St. George's University School of Medicine.

I visited St. George's University, whose students and officials, Lorde pointed out, later denied that they were ever in danger. The school, which is no longer just a medical school but covers other disciplines, is an island unto itself, with its many salmon-colored buildings, large water tanks, security personnel, and buses. All over the campus are breathtaking views of True Blue Bay, where the Caribbean Sea and the Atlantic Ocean meet.

If Reagan was so interested in seeing democracy flourish in the Caribbean, Lorde wondered, why did the US government support Haiti's dictators François and Jean-Claude Duvalier and their repressive regimes? She also mentioned Puerto Rico.

In 1897, she wrote, "U.S. Marines landed in Puerto Rico to fight the Spanish-American War. They never left." Like Dominica, Barbuda, and the US Virgin Islands, Puerto Rico was devastated by Hurricanes Irma and Maria.

At that time, I had not been to Puerto Rico either. I had only visited it in books, particularly through the eyes of young Esmeralda Santiago in her memoir, *When I Was Puerto Rican*. I imagined the guavas—which she taught other readers and me to eat at the beginning of her book—being no longer able to grow, the fields they came from deep in the countryside flattened, and the families that farmed them struggling to stay alive without food or clean water.

After the hurricanes, I watched an interview with the mayor of San Juan, Carmen Yulín Cruz Soto, and heard echoes of Audre Lorde in her voice.

"There is nothing that unites people more anywhere in the world than injustice," the mayor said. "We have to get food; we have to get water, or else we are being condemned to a slow death. It may be easy to try to disregard us. It may be easy because we are a US territory and a colony of the United States. But we're a people, damn it."

"We are a people" is what we have been saying for generations to colonizers, invaders, and imperialists hell-bent on destroying us. And now more than ever, Mother Nature, too. The blessings of our islands are also our curse. Our geography gives us the year-round sun and beautiful beaches, but increasingly, in the age of extreme weather and climate change, we are on the front line of destruction. The Arawak and Taíno might have said we are a people, even as they died trying to prove it. We have even inherited the word for hurricane, *huracán*, from them.

"Much has been terribly lost in Grenada," Lorde wrote at the end of her 1983 visit, "but not all—not the spirit of the people."

The spirit of the people is also captured in a poem I have been carrying with me for years before coming to Grenada. It was written by the Grenadian poet, short story writer, and novelist Merle Collins.

"We speak," she wrote in "Because the Dawn Breaks!," "for the same reason that the thunder frightens the child . . . that the lightning startles the tree . . ."

The people of the Caribbean speak, she wrote, because we "were not born to be your vassals."

Baldwin

In "Notes for a Hypothetical Novel," an address delivered at San Francisco State College on October 22, 1960, and later published in the essay collection *Nobody Knows My Name*, James Baldwin pretended he was writing a novel in front of an audience.

"Let's pretend," he said, "that I want to write a novel concerning the people or some of the people with whom I grew up, and since we are only playing let us pretend it's a very long novel. I want to follow a group of lives almost from the time they open their eyes on the world until some point of resolution, say, marriage, or childbirth, or death."

Baldwin had already published *Go Tell It on the Mountain* seven years earlier, so it appeared that he was not referring to his best-known and first novel. In other talks and essays, he'd laid out some ideas about what made an unsuccessful novel, citing problems like too neat a frame, sentimentality, and facile lessons and solutions. The novel he was referring to in the speech, though, he claimed, was both "unwritten and probably unwritable." Neither was it meant to be a "long, warm, toasty" novel. "This hypothetical book is aiming at something more implacable than that. . . . The social realities with which these people, the people I remember, whether they knew it or not, were really contending can't be left out of the novel without falsifying their experience."

As the speech continued, a boy emerged in Baldwin's hypothetical novel. The boy had abandoned the church he'd grown up in to smoke cigarettes and have sex. He was rejected by the community and died of tuberculosis a year and a half later. This boy was not the only casualty of the church's censure. A young woman lost her mind and ended up in a mental hospital. Still, Baldwin refused to limit his novel to a roster of disasters.

"The imagination of a novelist has everything to do with what happens to his material," he said. As the speech neared its end, however, it became clear that the two novels Baldwin had already written (*Go Tell It on the Mountain* and *Giovanni's Room*) and the ones he had yet to write were part of a colossal, deliberate oeuvre. *Go Tell It on the Mountain* was only his first attempt.

Initially titled *Crying Holy*, *Go Tell It on the Mountain* was written after Baldwin gave up being a youth preacher and left the church to become a writer. He worked on the book for more than ten years, including while he was living in Greenwich Village and Paris, and he only managed to finish it in 1952, after he'd moved to Loèche-les-Bains, a village in the Swiss Alps.

In a 1961 interview with the American broadcaster and oral historian Studs Terkel, Baldwin remembered thinking he might never finish the novel. But then he realized that one of the reasons he couldn't finish was that he was ashamed of where it came from.

"I was ashamed . . . of life in the church," he told Terkel, "and ashamed of my father, and ashamed of the blues, and ashamed of jazz, and of course ashamed of watermelon. . . . all of these stereotypes that the country afflicts on Negroes: that we all eat watermelon; that we all do nothing but sing the blues. . . . Well, I was afraid of all that and I ran from it."

He could only complete the novel once he stopped running.

Given the title, one might expect the novel's epigraph to be the refrain of the African American spiritual: "Go, tell it on the mountain / Over the hills and everywhere / Go, tell it on the mountain / That Jesus Christ is born." After all, this song has been sung by preachers, Christmas carolers, civil rights marchers, and famous gospel singers since it was cataloged by the Fisk professor John Wesley Work Jr. in 1907. However, the epigraph is from the Book of Revelation (22:17), an invitation to sinners to redeem themselves through Christ's symbolic bride, the Church.

> And the Spirit and the bride say, Come.
> And let him that hearest say, Come.
> And let him that is athirst come.
> And whosoever will, let him take the water of life freely.

Go Tell It on the Mountain is framed around the twenty-four hours that make up John Grimes's fourteenth birthday. The day begins on a sour note when John mistakenly thinks no one remembers. But his mother does remember, and she gives him some money, which he uses to explore the city for the day.

John's stops at different New York City landmarks outside Harlem allow Baldwin (who was, like John, a child of the Great Migration, the mass movement of more than six million African Americans from the rural South to urban centers in the northern United States) to paint a vivid picture of nineteen-thirties New York and the mixed feelings the city evokes in young John. For example, Baldwin writes of John seeing the city's skyline from a hill in Central Park:

> *He did not know why, but there arose in him an exultation and a sense of power, and he ran up the hill like an engine, or a madman, willing to throw himself headlong into the city that glowed before him.*

At the end of the day, though, John finds himself in familiar territory, in the fiery bosom of the Temple of the Fire Baptized church. Eventually, with the urging of the saints, he is entranced by the Holy Ghost and repents at the mourner's bench, the threshing floor. The section of the novel devoted to John's conversion, reckoning, and transformation electrifies the story's final pages like the service must have rocked the Temple of the Fire Baptized that night. Baldwin, who both experienced and induced such ecstasy himself as a youth minister, does such a great job of capturing what it's like to be enraptured that I always find myself trembling a little while I'm reading the scene. It also reminds me of many nights spent in the pews of my uncle's church in Haiti, watching so many people become overcome with the

Holy Ghost that they had to be picked up from the church aisle and carried to the altar while gyrating in the arms of a group of deacons who'd occasionally catch a kick in the stomach or face during this sanctified recovery mission.

On the threshing floor, John has visions, some like the ones he'd imagined earlier in the city, but they are even more fraught and glorious and even further out of reach.

"Lord, I ain't / No stranger now!" the congregation sings as they rise to their feet.

In "Down at the Cross: Letter from a Region in My Mind," published in his essay collection *The Fire Next Time*, Baldwin writes about undergoing a similar experience: "I underwent, during the summer that I became fourteen, a prolonged religious crisis. I use the word 'religious' in the common, and arbitrary, sense, meaning that I then discovered God, His saints and angels, and His blazing Hell."

The blazing hell is one that neither Baldwin nor John could ignore, a place much like the city where John feels both invisible and reviled. The summer Baldwin turned fourteen was full of police violence, from which he was not spared. Even when he was younger, at ten years old, he was frisked and verbally assaulted by some police officers who left him on the ground, on his back, in the street. He was a child, but they could not see it. His young Black body was already considered menacing, a threat.

"It was absolutely clear that the police would whip you and take you in as long as they could get away with it," Baldwin wrote. Incidents like this were, in part, what led Baldwin to the church in the first place.

"Some went on wine or whiskey or the needle, and are still on it. And others, like me, fled into the church," he wrote.

"Because I am an American writer," Baldwin stated in his San Francisco State address, "my subject and my material inevitably has to be a handful of incoherent people in an incoherent country." This incoherence, he says, is analogous to having a friend who's keeping the mother he's murdered in his closet, and though we know about it, we refuse to talk about it. This is what the best novels do, unbury the dead, or at least break down the doors and let the skeletons out.

As the hypothetical-novel speech wound down, it became apparent, too, that Baldwin was speaking about more than a novel. He was also talking about a country that was supposed to offer more opportunities to John Grimes and to Baldwin than it had to their ancestors.

"A country is only as strong as the people who make it up and the country turns into what the people want it to become," he said. "Now, this country is going to be transformed. It will not be transformed by an act of God, but by all of us, by you and me."

García Márquez

At the beginning of *One Hundred Years of Solitude*, Macondo's patriarch, José Arcadio Buendía, wants to move the idyllic yet isolated community he founded to another, more accessible location. And, since no one else wants to go with him, he decides that he and his wife, Úrsula, and their son should leave.

"We will not leave," his wife says, reminding him that Macondo was their son's birthplace.

"We have still not had a death," he tells her. "A person does not belong to a place until there is someone dead under the ground." His wife replies, "If I have to die for the rest of you to stay here, I will die."

This was the first thing that came to mind when I heard, on April 17, 2014, that Gabriel García Márquez had died. For anyone who's been forced, or has chosen, to start a new life in a new place, that scene provides at least two possible markers by which one can belong. By Úrsula's definition, it is through life. By her husband's, it is through death.

When my older daughter, Mira, was born in Miami in 2005, I remember thinking that, after nearly a quarter century of living in the United States, I finally had an unbreakable bond with the place. When my father, who had once imagined that he'd be buried in Haiti, was buried in Queens, New York, a few months after Mira's birth, those ties became even stronger. After all, if we're pushed out, we can always take the living with us. However, the dead can prove less mobile.

In October 2003, I was invited to participate in a PEN America tribute to Gabriel García Márquez. The title of the evening was "Gabriel García Márquez: Everyday Magic." The great man himself wasn't there. He was already ill, I think. Among the other speakers that evening were the writers Francisco Goldman, Salman Rushdie, Paul Auster, and William Kennedy—and former president Bill Clinton, on video. That he counted Bill Clinton and Fidel Castro among his friends astounded and outraged the woman sitting beside me. The writers, however, focused on his work.

Francisco Goldman mentioned a study that had found that, aside from the Bible, García Márquez's *Love in the Time of Cholera* was the book you were most likely to find in possession of Latin American sex workers. Salman Rushdie pointed out the many similarities between García Márquez's world and the one where he'd grown up, in India.

"It was a world in which there were colossal differences between the very poor and the very rich and not much in between; also a world bedeviled by dictators and corruption," Rushdie said.

Like many of the other speakers that night, Rushdie rejected the idea that García Márquez's fiction was "fantastic."

And I agreed. Having been born and lived in a profoundly spiritual and extraordinarily resourceful Haiti, I often found what might seem magical to others entirely plausible. What seems implausible is a lifetime of absolute normalcy, a world without assassinations, coups d'état, invasions, occupations, poverty, dictators, earthquakes, or hurricanes. I had always felt that García Márquez's short stories often took a back seat to his longer works and that his deadpan dark humor was not discussed often enough, so that night, I read an excerpt from one of my favorites of his short stories, "One of These Days."

In the story, the town mayor, a military torturer, shows up in absolute agony at the office of Aurelio Escovar, "a dentist without a degree." The mayor is in so much pain from an abscess in his mouth that he's unable to shave half his beard. Yet he still announces that he will shoot the dentist if he refuses to help him. Finally, seeing an opportunity to avenge the recent massacre of twenty of his neighbors, the dentist tricks the mayor into letting him pull the diseased tooth out without anesthesia. But the dentist does not quite get the revenge he seeks. When he asks the mayor whether to send the bill to him personally or to the town, the mayor exclaims, "It's the same damn thing."

Like so many others, this story shows how García Márquez also depicted some common yet unbearable daily realities. Still, I keep returning to José Arcadio Buendía and his desire to leave. José Arcadio had hoped to guide his people toward the "invisible north," only to discover that Macondo was entirely surrounded by water. But he would not despair. There was more work to do. And he had not yet experienced death and the light rain of tiny yellow flowers that would fall to mark his passing. He had not yet seen that silent storm and the cushion of petals that had to be cleared with rakes and shovels as his funeral procession went by. And perhaps neither had Gabo until he died.

Morrison and Marshall

I learned of Toni Morrison's death at sunrise, and Paule Marshall's a week later, at sunset. News of Ms. Morrison's transition, as many of my bereaved friends called it, quickly spread on social media and in the international press. Word of Ms. Marshall's passing— another term many of us used to soften the blow of both deaths— was disseminated more slowly. (Ms. Morrison was eighty-eight; Ms. Marshall was ninety.) In Ms. Marshall's case, her death initially felt, as Ms. Morrison wrote in her 1984 essay "Rootedness: The Ancestor as Foundation," like "a very personal grief and a personal statement done among people you trust." I heard about it from a journalist who emailed me to confirm that Ms. Marshall had, indeed, died on Monday, August 12, 2019.

I knew both women and was blessed to have spent some time in their company. Before I ever saw them in the flesh, though, I was in awe of their words.

I first encountered Ms. Morrison's words in "Rootedness" in Mari Evans's *Black Women Writers (1950–1980): A Critical Evaluation*, in which Ms. Morrison wrote, "It seems to me interesting to evaluate Black literature on what the writer does with the presence of an ancestor." Ancestors, she wrote, "are not just parents, they are sort of timeless people."

Growing up, I had been told similar things by members of my family. I had been assured that our ancestors were always with us, if no longer in body, always in spirit. Ms. Marshall, too, referred to herself as an "unabashed ancestor worshipper." She could have been describing the women who'd raised me when she wrote in her essay "From the Poets in the Kitchen":

> *I grew up among poets. Now they didn't look like poets—*
> *whatever that breed is supposed to look like. Nothing about*

them suggested that poetry was their calling. They were just
a group of ordinary housewives and mothers, my mother
included, who dressed in a way (shapeless housedresses,
dowdy felt hats and long, dark, solemn coats) that made
it impossible for me to imagine they had ever been young.

Ms. Marshall further wrote of the women in her family, "They never put pen to paper except to write occasionally to their relatives in Barbados. 'I take my pen in hand hoping these few lines will find you in health as they leave me fair for the time being,' was the way their letters invariably began."

My parents' letters began similarly, except we would add *grace à Dieu* (thanks be to God).

To honor this connection and the other ways I felt seen in Ms. Marshall's short stories and many of her novels—including *Brown Girl, Brownstones, The Chosen Place, The Timeless People, Praisesong for the Widow,* and *Daughters,* among others—I draped my words around hers in the epilogue of my 1995 story collection *Krik? Krak!*:

Are there women who both cook and write? Kitchen poets,
they call them. They slip phrases into their stew and wrap
meaning around their pork before frying it. They make
narrative dumplings.

Krik? Krak! was my second published book, but the one I first began writing parts of soon after I'd read both the Evans anthology and Ms. Marshall's essay about kitchen poets. As the oldest child and only daughter of parents who were always working, I often cooked for my family, and I worried that I might not be able to cook and write equally. This often crossed my mind when I had the honor of breaking bread with Ms. Morrison and Ms. Marshall.

After *Krik? Krak!* was published, Ms. Marshall called me to ask if I wanted to teach at New York University, where she had a permanent position. Before the official job interview, she invited me for tea at her apartment overlooking Washington Square Park. We discussed the job a bit. Then we talked about Haiti, where she lived on and off while she was married to her second husband, a Haitian businessman. After overcoming my shyness, I asked her how she'd found such a fabulous apartment so close to the university. She chuckled, then said, "When I came for my job interview, the dean asked me where I wanted to live. I looked around his lavish office and said, 'Something like this will do.'"

We laughed. She had a vibrant and youthful laugh. Even though I knew that as an adjunct I was getting neither a lavish office nor a fabulous apartment, I took the job. That fall, she hosted a reading series and invited me to read in it, along with the novelists Glenville Lovell and A. J. Verdelle. She encouraged me to speak to her if I needed anything. Not wanting to bother her, I only took up that offer once when one of my white male students was particularly disruptive in our majority women of color class. I had spoken to the young man, but everything had stayed the same, so I went to Ms. Marshall for advice. I suspected she had taken up the issue herself because the young man reverted to regular writing-workshop banter soon after our conversation and retreated from personal attacks.

The first time I broke bread with Ms. Morrison was in the fall of 2006, in one of the cafés at the Louvre, in Paris, where she was in residence for a month. A few months earlier, her assistant, Rene Boatman, had called to ask if I would join Ms. Morrison and a group of other writers, dancers, and filmmakers, including Charles Burnett and Michael Ondaatje, at the Louvre. When the call came, I had just been diagnosed with pneumonia and was still nursing my infant daughter, Mira. So I told Ms. Boatman I couldn't go. Besides, I thought they'd made a mistake. I felt undeserving.

The next day, Ms. Morrison called, and I told her about my infant and my pneumonia, and she said, "You're not going to have pneumonia for a year, and your baby's going to grow. So tell me what you'll need to be there."

I made what I believed was an unreasonable request, but it was what kept me afloat. I told her that my husband, who worked remotely, and I needed my mother and mother-in-law to help with the baby while I participated in the planned events.

She said, "Done." A few months later, my family and I were in Paris, in an apartment near the Louvre. Seeing Paris had been a lifelong dream for my mother, and though we had gone on many other trips together, we had yet to make it there. When she met Ms. Morrison at the opening event, my mother thanked her profusely. Ms. Morrison smiled mischievously at both my mother and my mother-in-law and told them to go out alone now and then and enjoy the city.

There were many more moments of extraordinary kindness afforded to me by Ms. Marshall and Ms. Morrison. In Paris, Ms. Morrison had given me a gorgeous hairpin—like the ones she sometimes wore. The next time I saw her at an event, I felt terrible for not having it on, then confessed that I'd had to stash the hairpin away because my daughter loved it so much that she kept trying to eat it. The next time I saw her, at another event, she gave me another pin. "Your baby can keep the first one," she said.

Ms. Marshall wrote me a thoughtful condolence note after my uncle died, in immigration custody, in 2004. In 2007, Ms. Morrison was at the National Book Awards ceremony, where my book about my uncle's death, *Brother, I'm Dying*, was a finalist. At the end of the night, as my family and I were leaving the hall, someone stopped me and told me that Ms. Morrison wanted to speak to me. Ms. Morrison then walked up to our group, which included my mother. We all chatted about the evening, then Ms. Morrison leaned over and said, "I've never won one of these, either. Only the one for all my books." She was referring to her 1996 National Book Foundation Medal for Distinguished Contribution to American Letters.

At the dinner, before a talk I gave for her eponymous lecture series at Princeton in March 2008, as soon as we sat down to eat, she asked me if I had been well compensated. When I told her I was, she smiled that broad, generous smile, then said, "Good. I don't want them being cheap in my name."

During these brief and sometimes longer interactions with Ms. Morrison and Ms. Marshall, I saw myself as lucky but not necessarily singular. At times, I felt like a representative of all their younger writer admirers, particularly those who enjoyed both the person and the work. And I sometimes worried as the years went on that one day I might have to share these stories about them while I was weighed down with sadness. I guess you might call that feeling, to use Ms. Morrison's words from her 1973 novel, *Sula*, the "sheer good fortune to miss somebody long before they leave you."

Ms. Morrison was still writing toward the end of her life—she would often say so at public events—but Ms. Marshall had not published a book since her slim 2009 memoir, *Triangular Road*. Every now and then, when I tried to reach Ms. Marshall and never heard back, I would imagine her writing yet another epic novel that would take me weeks to read. Ms. Marshall often said that she was a notoriously slow writer. I kept hoping that she was just being slow.

Triangular Road, adapted from a series of lectures Ms. Marshall delivered at Harvard University in 2005, begins with a scene in which Ms. Marshall receives an invitation to go on a European speaking tour with the writer Langston Hughes.

"The invitation in hand, I stood dumbstruck for the longest time," she wrote. "Langston Hughes! None other than the poet laureate of Black America had chosen me to accompany him on a cultural tour of Europe! Me a mere fledging of a writer, with only one novel and a collection of stories published to date! Why would someone of his stature so much as consider a novice like myself?"

This also describes how I often felt in both Ms. Morrison's and Ms. Marshall's company. I wouldn't even allow myself to address them by their first names out of respect and reverence. Ms. Marshall referred to Langston Hughes as Mr. Hughes during her talks and throughout her memoir.

"For me," she wrote, "he was a loving taskmaster, mentor, teacher, griot, literary sponsor and treasured elder friend. Decades have passed since his death in 1967 and I still miss him."

In the 1970s, Ms. Marshall and Ms. Morrison were members of The Sisterhood, a New York–based Black women writers' group whose members included Ntozake Shange, Louise Meriwether, June Jordan, and Alice Walker. Perhaps Ms. Morrison and Ms. Marshall had some extraordinarily insightful discussions before, during, and after those meetings, chats that I wish I could have eavesdropped on. Maybe they are still having some of those chats now, with Lorraine Hansberry, Audre Lorde, James Baldwin, and Gabriel García Márquez, among others.

When I was asked to speak at Ms. Morrison's memorial service at the Cathedral of St. John the Divine in New York City on November 21, 2019, a service that also included the writers Jesmyn Ward, Ta-Nehisi Coates, Michael Ondaatje, and Oprah Winfrey, I began to see her and aspects of her work everywhere.

I saw her in bleak and sunny skies. I saw her in daisy trees.

I saw her on benches by the road. I heard her voice in church hymns, spirituals, and jazz tunes, because she was, as she wrote of Jadine in *Tar Baby*, "not only a woman but a sound . . . a world and a way of being in it."

I kept seeing her, too, in shiny, beautiful hairpins woven through gray locks. Each time she'd given me one of those hairpins, I felt as though she was sharing pieces of her infinite crown with me. I felt her presence in her sister writer friends, Sonia Sanchez and Nikki Giovanni, and Black women writers closer to my age and younger, like Jesmyn Ward and Tayari Jones. Though she carried a particular strand of genius in every single cell of her body, she had constantly reminded us that it is indeed not scarce and that we, too, could skillfully, beautifully, and politically tell our stories. ("If there is a book that you want to read, but it hasn't been written yet, then you must write it.") This had made it so much easier to tremble less in her physical presence. Because "quiet as it's kept," she half giggled when she laughed and had a twinkle in her eye when she was in the presence of someone whose company she enjoyed. She drank vodka on a cold day—the really good stuff— and smoked cigarettes. At the Louvre, she was the literary giant that is Toni Morrison, but she was also Chloe Wofford, and she allowed me, in brief, privileged moments, to see them both, for which I will always be grateful. Her work was, of course, sublime. We do not just read it, we experience it. She gave us both lullabies and battle cries. She turned pain into flesh and brought spirits to life. She urged us to be dangerously free. She gave this foreigner a home. Her work has carried me through adolescence and marriage, parenthood, and orphanhood. I have recited and paraphrased her sentences to myself while cradling the tiny bodies of my newborn daughters ("They get bigger, older, but grown? What's that supposed to mean?") and the skeletal faces of my dying parents ("Soft as cream"). I hoped that, like Baby

Suggs, they too would die soft as cream. And I came to think of her, as she wrote·in *The Bluest Eye*, not only as a friend of my mind but as someone who "does not want me to die."

"Death is as natural as life," she wrote. "And you sure did live in this world!" I said in the church that day. Some called her Sister, *Soror*. Others called her Teacher, Editor, Beloved, and Mentor. "We still call you by those names," I said, "but now we also call you Timeless. We now call you Ancestor."

I remember visiting her home in Grand View, New York, in 2016. We had spent the morning revisiting, for a documentary called *The Foreigner's Home*, the month she was in residence at the Louvre. That day in her house, we talked about slavery, racism, immigration, political art, Hurricane Katrina, breakdancing, and hip-hop, particularly Kendrick Lamar, for whom she expressed her admiration. When it came time for me to leave, it was snowing outside, a sheet of snow so thick that it blocked her view of the Hudson right below. She was sitting by the window at her kitchen table with the winter afternoon light and shadows of snowflakes dancing across her face. Before leaving, I leaned down to kiss the top of her head, which was covered with a beautiful black-and-white scarf. At that moment, I felt, once again, the sheer good fortune of already missing her long before she was gone. My kiss on the top of her head created a spark that startled us both, with a surge of static electricity from the rug beneath our feet.

"Goodbye, Ms. Morrison," I said.

"Goodbye," she said. Then she added, "I'm going to rest now."

"Dying was OK because it was sleep," she has written.

In *Tar Baby*, a doubter is told, "The world will always be there—while you sleep it will be there." This, of course, is also true for her, I reminded her at the memorial.

The world will be here, though certainly less rich, or full. It will still be there, though, while you rest. And when you're done resting, remember, they are waiting in the hills for you. Just as Jardine's ancestors were waiting for her in *Tar Baby*. They are all waiting in the hills for you, a hill full of benches by the roads where the daisy trees plentifully grow. They are all waiting there for you, Maya Angelou, Langston Hughes, Nina Simone, Chinua Achebe, Billie Holiday, Josephine Baker, Audre Lorde, Lorraine Hansberry, James Baldwin, Gabriel García Márquez, Paule Marshall, and so many others. They are all waiting in the hills for you. So go ahead and join them after your well-earned rest, I told her from the church pulpit. Hopefully, she will also be waiting for me when my time comes.

This Is My Body

1

Two days before Christmas 2017, I headed to a popular mall—Aventura Mall—not far from my home to get my then twelve-year-old daughter Mira her first cell phone. The line to drive into the mall was endless. It was, I suspected, filled with people like me, who could no longer get anything online that would be delivered before Christmas. The line at the store was also long, but not as long as the winding lane of cars heading for the exit of the five-story parking lot after I purchased the phone.

I'd felt lucky to have found a spot on the top floor when I arrived, but at the pace the cars were moving, I worried that I might still be sitting in my car on Christmas morning. Then, just as I neared the second floor, dozens of people raced past my car. Among the many screams and voices I heard was a woman calling for someone named Jackson. In the surreal way that one's mind works at a time like this, I remember thinking, for a second, that she was calling the King of Pop, Michael Jackson. Later I realized that had I been shot to death then and there, my final thought on this earth would have been of Michael Jackson.

The crowd rushing past my car and the other cars stuck in the parking lot made driving out impossible.

"What's going on?" I shouted at the people sprinting past.

The same question echoed from the mouths of other drivers both in front of and behind me.

"There's a shooter in the mall," many of the fleeing said.

The pace of events quickened as people began to shout "Run!" even as they were already running. It was obvious then that I too would have to run. The cars were at a standstill. Many of the drivers ahead of me had already abandoned their vehicles. I quickly turned off my car, then put the keys and the phone in my purse. Then I heard a series of loud explosions. To my panicked ears, it sounded like bombs were going off nearby. Suddenly there were many more of us sprinting, running, dashing, more abandoned cars, and more parents screaming their children's names. It was hard to tell, as I wove my way through a crowd of fleeing people and unmoving cars, whether I was escaping or heading toward these explosions.

My adrenaline took over and I ran down the ramp until I was on the ground floor and outside. At the exit were several heavily armed police officers headed in the direction I'd just come from. I was still hearing the explosions, which made me wonder whether the active shooter, or shooters, might not also be snipers who could be waiting to pick off those fleeing from the many stores surrounding us. I spotted a bush on the side of the parking structure and took cover there. The bush was part of a low hedge that was meant to soften the look of the concrete. I squeezed myself in between that hedge and the wall to catch my breath.

People were still running, still fleeing the mall. More police and emergency vehicles were coming in too. After a few minutes behind the hedge, I joined a group of shoppers heading toward a footbridge that led to the main road outside the mall. Everyone was out of breath, all of us, walking again—and not running—for the first time since fleeing the mall. Then the flood of cell phone calls began. Many were still frantic. Some had left behind loved ones, who as far as they knew were caught up in a bloodbath or a massacre.

My husband and two daughters were at a holiday theme park called Santa's Enchanted Forest. I texted him to let him know I was safe. I then entered the words *Aventura Mall* in the Advanced Search box on Twitter, now X, and the first tweet I saw was written by Jacqueline Charles, a *Miami Herald* reporter, who happened to be in the mall and was hiding inside a storeroom closet with dozens of other people. I called my niece who lived nearby. When she and her husband arrived, I got in their car, collapsed in the back seat, and burst into tears. I was already counting the numbers in my head. Judging from the size of the mall and the booming explosions I'd heard, I believed that dozens of people had already died. I imagined the headlines and the breaking news banners. This one, I thought, would probably be called "The Christmas Massacre."

Though there had been and would be other shootings resulting from arguments at the mall, this one turned out to be a hoax. Some young people had perpetrated the hoax with an app that made the sounds of gunshots and bomb detonations, which were then amplified by speakers. In similar hoaxes throughout Florida malls the following week, firecrackers were used to cause panic so that criminals could rob stores.

When I first learned about the potential massacre being a hoax, I felt lucky, but also angry. Then I began making jokes. My greatest shame, I told my niece, would have been dying clutching that dammed phone. As soon as I was reunited with my family, my mother-in-law reminded me how when I learned that my husband and daughters were going to spend the afternoon at Santa's Enchanted Forest, I had worried that, much like the mall, a place filled with hundreds of distracted children and adults might be, in modern terrorism or mass shooter speak, a soft target. Still, both my husband and I had kept to our plans. After all, these things always seemed to happen in other places, and to other people.

In recent years—particularly with the young activists who emerged after the February 14, 2018, mass shooting at Marjory Stoneman Douglas High School in Parkland, Florida—we have had many detailed accounts of what it's like to actually survive one of those massacres. The grace of the young Parkland survivors, their eloquence, their efforts to include less privileged youth— among them young people of color whose communities are chronically and disproportionately affected by gun violence—have been especially eye opening. As one of Mira's teachers said when we went to our local March for Our Lives rally, the day before Mira's thirteenth birthday, my daughters' generation has lived in great proximity to graphic, vivid trauma due to gun violence. They also have enough tools, including social media, to share real-time accounts of the shootings and the aftermath with the rest of us. Our children not only read about dying violently, or see it online, or act it out, as some do, in sadistic video games. They are also being trained to expect dying while planning how to avoid it. One of the signs I found most heartbreaking at our local March for Our Lives rally was carried by an African American girl who looked like she was around ten, which was then my younger daughter Leila's age.

The sign simply read, "LET US GROW UP!"

In the days that followed, I thought of my experience at Aventura Mall as a kind of drill, not unlike the ones carried out at my daughters' school and at many other schools around the country. Soon after the Marjory Stoneman Douglas High School shootings, each of my daughters came home describing her own experience of the active shooter drill at school. Leila was told to hide under her desk, which, even she acknowledged, is wooden and small and would not protect her from an assault rifle. Mira was told that if she was in the hallway with the active shooter nearby, she should find an unlocked classroom and run inside. Since her class had been advised to lock the door, I told her to run instead to the nearest bathroom or supply closet and take cover there. I hoped I hadn't given her potentially deadly advice.

2

I spent a lot of time thinking about suddenly dying after that day at Aventura Mall, but even before that, since my mother died of ovarian cancer in October 2014. Part of my job as a writer is to wrestle with mortality, both my own and that of others. I do this, in part, by writing about fictional people I give life to, throw untold atrocities at, then either redeem or destroy. In my own life, one way I wrestle with mortality is by keeping a pocket-size notebook with a list of instructions and counsel for my daughters, ranging from what they might call cringe ("Do not ever underestimate how awesome you are") to the spiritual ("Keep some element of faith in your life. You saw how your grandmother's faith brought her such solace and comfort as she was dying"). This, too, I took from my mother. The day she died, on the nightstand by her bed I found an advice-filled cassette created for my three brothers and me. On the tape, she told us not to be too sad, since she'd lived a long and fulfilling life, as well as what I should wear to her funeral: a long-sleeved black dress, a hat, no open-toe shoes. That cassette, I now realize, is one of the ways she resisted dying.

As a terminal cancer patient, my mother understood how not to die, even when you *must* die. Her tranquil yet firm voice on that cassette proves it. She knew we would be listening to her long after she was gone. She still wanted to parent us from the grave.

At the end of my mother's life, when we were constantly telling each other stories, I told her how I'd once heard that a kind of amber-colored rice we loved is said to have come to our part of the world from the African continent because an enslaved woman had hidden some grains of it in her hair. I'd also heard that rice had been brought to the Caribbean by European enslavers to supplement the meager diet of the enslaved. However, we preferred the story of the woman with the rice in her hair.

"You mean her scalp was a garden?" my mother asked incredulously, even as her own scalp became more exposed as a side effect of chemotherapy.

The woman with the rice in her hair, I realize, was already imagining a future in which she would exist only as an ancestor. Perhaps she already knew that one day she would become a *lejann*, and a food and body story.

3

The father of a friend used to tell her, as she enjoyed what he considered a bit too much food, that she was digging her grave with her teeth. I often think of this supposed oral grave digging when I am with incarcerated people. In the prisons and immigration detention centers that I have visited, food and body stories come up regularly. Many Haitian immigration detainees see the terrible food they are fed at the most inconvenient hours—sometimes at four in the morning for breakfast and four in the afternoon for dinner—as *manje dekouraje*, food meant to punish them, and encourage them to beg to be deported, and later tell others not to come.

The food would neither "stay up nor down," one woman told me in early 2002 when I met her in the south Florida hotel that had been turned into a holding facility for women and children who'd come to Miami by boat from Haiti. These women either vomited this food or it gave them diarrhea. Six of them lived in one hotel room. Some were forced to sleep on the floor. Not only did these women have no control over what they were putting in their bodies, but it was making them sick, and the sickness was further dehumanizing them.

During my teenage years, in the early 1980s, my parents used to take me to visit Haitian refugees and asylum seekers at a detention center near the Brooklyn Navy Yard. The men there believed that hormones in the detention center food were making them grow breasts, a condition known as gynecomastia. In October 1987, thirty Haitian men who had been detained at Miami's Krome detention center filed a civil suit against the US government claiming that they'd developed gynecomastia while they were at Krome. The lawsuit revealed that the gynecomastia might have been caused by the detention center's use of insecticides, particularly a type meant for animals, and Kwell, a harsh antiscabies and lice cream, which was given to Haitian detainees to use daily as a body lotion. Other research, however, found clear links between diet and gynecomastia, and the men remained convinced that the detention center food had something to do with it. Despite all this, a jury found the US government, their jailer, not liable.

One of the ways my immigrant parents tried to immerse my brothers and me in American culture was to let us choose pizza, fried chicken, or hot dogs on Friday nights after eating rice and beans, plantains, and other Haitian dishes every other night of the week. My mother liked to tell my brothers and me that *sak vid pa kanpe* (empty sacks don't stand) and *se sa k nan vant ou ki pa w* (only what's in your belly is yours). She often told us these things right before we went to someone else's house for lunch or dinner. The ultimate lesson in those maxims and proverbs was to never show up somewhere too hungry. You never knew when your hosts would be ready to feed you, and you must not seem too famished, too desperate, too *empty* when they do. And if by any chance your arrival at someone's house happens to coincide with a meal to which you were not previously invited, you must refuse the food you are offered, even if you are starving. Otherwise it will seem as though you purposely showed up for that meal and that would make you seem calculatingly greedy, *visye*.

Meals eaten in desperation or under distress of course end up being memorable. The choice of pre-execution meals generates so much interest that they are often mentioned, along with the final words spoken by the executed, in postmortem press conferences. The most legendary final meal is the Last Supper. We have no account of what else was consumed at the Last Supper besides unleavened bread and wine, which Jesus offered to his disciples—including the ones who would renounce and betray him, by saying, "Take, eat; this is my body." Then, "Drink, this is my blood."

I think of all this, too, when I hear about people who have nothing in their stomach of their choosing, people who have no choice but to swallow food they despise, and people who are fed against their will while they are jailed. Algerian-born Lakhdar Boumediene was living in Bosnia in October 2001 when he was accused of participating in a terrorist plot. He was cleared by Bosnian authorities after a thorough investigation, yet was turned over to US authorities, who renditioned him to Guantánamo, where he was a prisoner from 2002 to 2009. In a 2017 opinion piece in the *New Republic*, he wrote about a monthlong hunger strike, which he started in December 2006:

> *I stopped eating not because I wanted to die, but because I could not keep living without doing something to protest the injustice of my treatment. They could lock me up for no reason and with no chance to argue my innocence. They could torture me, deprive me of sleep, put me in an isolation cell, control every single aspect of my life. But they couldn't make me swallow their food.*

In July 2013, the rapper and activist Yasiin Bey agreed to be force-fed in a manner similar to the way prisoners on hunger strike were being force-fed at Guantánamo Bay. Bey was strapped to a feeding chair that looked like an electric chair. His hands and feet and head were placed in restraints. A nasal gastric tube was forced through his nose, down the back of his throat, and into his stomach, a process the US military called enteral feeding. As Bey wriggled and twisted—to whatever extent he could—tears ran down his face. He coughed. He grunted. He pleaded with his "jailers," who were pressing the weight of their bodies on his chest and stomach, to stop.

"Please, please, don't," he begged.

After a minute or so, he was squirming so much that the tube fell out. The jailers put him in a choke hold to further restrain him and only stopped when he said, "This is me. Please stop. I can't do this anymore." Then he broke down and cried.

Had Bey been an actual prisoner, his jailers wouldn't have stopped until they were done force-feeding him. Those on hunger strike at Guantánamo Bay were fed like this twice a day, and for two hours each time, which led to Bey's demonstration as protest.

After being force-fed, those on hunger strike at Guantánamo would then have a mask placed over their mouths while their bodies processed the liquid nutritional supplement. Back in their "dry" cells, which meant there was no water in those cells, they were observed closely to see if they were vomiting. If they vomited the supplement, they were force-fed again. Many prisoners urinated and defecated on themselves in the chair. Prisoners who were fasting during Ramadan, the Muslim holy month, were force-fed before dawn and after sunset.

4

Sometimes when a person dies *a mò sibit*, suddenly with no previous sign of illness, the elders in my family will say that this person was "eaten." *Yo mange li*. They killed them by "eating" them. The *yo* (they) who's done the eating is often a person or a group of persons of ill will who have deployed some destructive force. We might never willingly offer ourselves to be "eaten" in this way (*Here is my body.*) unless we are noble to the point of being sacrificial or feel we have no choice.

In the early 1990s, before it became a military prison where terrorism suspects are detained indefinitely, the Guantánamo Naval Base in Cuba was used for warehousing over forty thousand Haitian asylum seekers who'd been intercepted by the US Coast Guard on the high seas after the coup d'état against President Jean-Bertrand Aristide.

Haitians were detained behind barbed wire and in four-foot-square cages. Families were separated. Some detainees were taken to an underground cage and tortured by the marines. Women were raped by US military officials, with at least one case leading to court-martial.

Because HIV-positive immigrants were banned from entering the United States at the time, HIV-positive asylum seekers were also held in Guantánamo. Over two hundred HIV-positive Haitians, led by Yolande Jean, a mother of two and Haitian political activist, started a hunger strike on January 23, 1993, that lasted ninety days. Yolande Jean told some visiting American journalists at that time: "We started the hunger strike so that this body could get spoiled and then the soul can go to God. Let me kill myself so my brothers and sisters can live."

In a letter addressed to her family, particularly to her sons, Hill and Jeff, Yolande Jean wrote:

> *To my family,*
> *Don't count on me anymore because I am lost in the struggle of life. Hill and Jeff, you don't have a mother anymore. Realize that you do not have a bad mother, only that life took me away. Goodbye, my children. Goodbye, my family. We will meet in another world.*

Yolande Jean was released from Guantánamo in May 1993 after her T cell count dangerously plunged below 200. She was reunited with her children in the United States. Half of the other HIV-positive hunger strikers died from the virus after being released.

"Sometimes surrendering to death is how you survive, but sometimes telling yourself that you will live, is how not to die," Yolande told me a few months after her release.

We were on the set of a video shoot for the title song of the 1993 AIDS courtroom drama *Philadelphia*, which was directed by the Academy Award–winning filmmaker Jonathan Demme. A passionate advocate for Haiti and Haitian refugees, Jonathan had followed Yolande's incarceration and hunger strike closely and recruited the actress Susan Sarandon to read Yolande's farewell letter at a March 1993 New York City protest, where Jonathan, Susan Sarandon, and the Reverend Jesse Jackson were arrested. I had worked for Jonathan as an assistant in the early 1990s, and he invited me to the set to translate for Yolande, whose body was plump and healthy again.

In the Bruce Springsteen video, the music star walks the streets of a mural-covered, children-filled, impoverished Philadelphia. Along his route, he crosses paths with a pensive Yolande Jean, who's watching a group of Black girls cheerfully jumping rope as Springsteen sings:

> *I was bruised and battered*
> *I couldn't tell what I felt*
> *I was unrecognizable to myself*

As I was sitting behind the hedge at Aventura Mall two days before Christmas 2017 I thought I heard this song playing somewhere in the distance. My mind raced backward and forward, thinking about all the people, including my children, who'd miss me most if I died. A few days later, I began writing a novel that opens in the mall. In the novel, people die, just as others have, or nearly died, at other times, in other malls, and just as I might have died that day. The novel's narrator, a survivor, also recalls some stories from her past. This is my body, she thinks, my blood.

PART 2

By the Time You Read This . . .

1

I suspected things might be getting serious when, at a memorial for an elderly friend who'd died long before COVID-19 was a pandemic, many of us tried to figure out how to greet one another. The scenario might have amused our friend, who'd died of natural causes, in the arms of his wife, at the age of ninety-three. His memorial was one of the last in-person gatherings on Florida International University's southwest campus, which soon moved to online learning. The remarks on our friend's life and work were preceded by a public service announcement reminding the sixty or so of us to avoid close physical contact.

"It will be hard not to touch. We're Haitians," we said to one another. We did what we could with elbow bumps, but there were occasional lapses into tearful hugs and kisses until someone jokingly suggested a butt bump, which a few of us tried, with mutual consent. We were not yet fully aware that there were people around the world dying painful and lonely deaths.

Saying that we're Haitians might also have been an acknowledgment of our past collisions with microbes. In October 2010, nine months after a magnitude 7.0 earthquake struck Port-au-Prince and the surrounding areas, Nepalese UN peacekeepers stationed in the north of Haiti released raw sewage from their base into one of Haiti's most used rivers, causing a cholera epidemic that killed ten thousand people and infected close to a million. During the weeks before Haiti had any COVID-19 cases, friends and family members there would text and WhatsApp-message me and others to tell us to watch out for the disease. It was a reversal, in which our fragility now seemed more significant than theirs.

"This, too, shall pass," one cousin kept writing, increasingly concerned as the number of COVID-19-related deaths rose in Florida. "I hope that all will be okay by the time you read this."

"I hope that by the time you read this . . ." So would end many notes and letters I used to write before email and text existed. If it was a letter to a sick friend, for example, I'd write, "I hope that by the time you read this, you're already feeling better." Because there was a delay between the time I had scribbled my handwritten note and put it in the mail and the time the person on the other end would receive it, I expected some change to have already occurred, some shift to have taken place, and I always hoped it would be for the better. I never thought to write, "Things might have really gone to hell by the time you read this." Time, I always wished, would improve terrible circumstances. This, too, I hoped, would pass.

Then my neighbor died. I saw the ambulance arrive. The red and blue strobes bounced off every glass surface on both sides of our block. She was eighty years old, and ambulances had come for her before. There was that time she broke her arm in her backyard and, already accustomed to arthritis pain, she treated herself until her movements led to other fractures. She stayed in the hospital for several days and then spent a few weeks at a rehab center.

She was among the first people my husband and I met when we moved to Miami's Little Haiti neighborhood eighteen years before. We had an avocado tree in our yard, and one day we saw her standing outside the gate looking at it. The gate had been "locked" with a metal coat hanger that allowed easy access to the avocado tree. For years, when the house was empty, everyone on our block could come into the yard to get avocados. Our buying the house changed that. My husband gave her some avocados. She suggested a few neighbors who had benefited from previous harvests. My husband gave them some, too.

"See," she told my husband, "I have made you popular on the block."

My neighbor died soon after our mourning rituals were taken away: the home visits, the festive wakes, the funerals, postburial repasts, and in-person memorial services. Mourning had become, like everything else, something to be done at a distance, an occasion that might prove too dangerous up close.

My husband walked to our neighbor's front yard after we first saw the ambulance lights through our bedroom window. Miami had become one of the epicenters of the pandemic. My two daughters, my mother-in-law, and I waited inside to avoid being exposed. My husband returned a few minutes after the ambulance pulled away. He said our neighbor had no pulse, but the emergency medical technician told our neighbor's daughter, who lived with her, that they would work on her mother on the way to the hospital. The daughter was told she wouldn't be allowed inside the hospital. My neighbor's death was not a COVID-19 death. She'd had gallbladder surgery and was in the hospital for two weeks. When she came home, she no longer had any appetite or thirst. I had visited her in the hospital during previous stays, but this time we were not even aware that she was sick. I suppose her daughter figured, why tell, since no one, including family members, could visit. When my mother died of ovarian cancer in our house, this neighbor came over to sit with us that night. She prayed with us when my mother was near death. We attended the same small church, and sometimes I gave her and her slightly younger sister a ride home. She loved to hand out cookies and hard candy to the kids at church. She cooed over my daughters when they were just a few days old.

Earlier that month, her daughter had organized a drive-by for her eightieth birthday. Over a dozen cars—she was the matriarch of a large family—streamed by her house. Her friends and family honked their horns while waving *Happy Birthday* banners and blasting loud celebratory music. We all went outside, wearing masks, to shout happy birthday from across the street. We watched as she swayed to the different types of music—hip-hop, Haitian konpa, gospel—played for her. She wore a beautiful pink suit with a Miss America–type sash across her chest. She looked overjoyed. She said her children had been planning a lavish party pre-COVID. They'd rented a banquet hall, and friends and family members were supposed to come from all over the world, including Haiti and the Bahamas, where she'd spent her youth.

I remembered my neighbor's description of her pre-COVID-19 birthday party plans. Her party sounded like a dream my mother-in-law had described to me a week before our neighbor died. There was a lavish banquet at church. People were singing and dancing, rejoicing that they could finally be together again. In dreams, a feast signifies death, my mother-in-law had explained. Might death be a cause for celebration in some other realm?

After our neighbor's death was confirmed, my mother-in-law and I walked over to her front yard and knocked on the window of her living room, where a family meeting was taking place. Our neighbor's daughter stood in the doorway and said, "My mother left us. She left us tonight."

I remember having to announce my mother's death over and over to friends. I recently had to do it again, years later, to an old friend I hadn't spoken to in some time.

"She's gone," I would say. "She's gone," leading some to think that my mother had left Miami while she was sick and returned to New York, where she'd spent most of her life.

As my mother-in-law and I stood in front of our neighbor's house, a sprinkle of rain began falling; it felt like the God our neighbor loved so much was weeping for her. We could not go inside and sit with her and her siblings, so we stood out in the rain for a few minutes and, while we were looking up at the daughter, kept muttering, "*Kondoleyans*. Sorry. We are so sorry. Very sorry."

Soon after my neighbor died, while I was sitting at dusk with my family at the beach near our home, I looked up at the sky and was in awe. The sky looked the most luminous I had ever seen. Swirls of cirrus, cumulus, and altostratus clouds appeared to have been set aflame by the Saharan dust sunset. The fact that dust from the Sahara Desert could be hovering over the sky in Miami reminded me that colors, like viruses, could mutate. It was as if the sky had become a colossal color field painting, with layers of hues and shades, pigments and shapes, dipping into the horizon.

What were these flaming skies trying to tell us? Aristotle thought that colors—which he linked to the four essential elements of earth, water, fire, and air—came to us directly from the heavens. Leonardo da Vinci observed that between shadows are other shadows. This phrase reminds me of the Haitian proverb *dèyè mòn gen mòn*, or beyond mountains are more mountains, which is something I overheard my neighbor saying to her younger sister more than once when I gave them a ride home from church.

In lieu of flowers, the family asked, via texts, that donations be made to an organization in Haiti that my neighbor had been supporting for decades. They also sent a Zoom link for the funeral.

I have always found comfort in some of the performative aspects of mourning: the covering of mirrors and other shiny surfaces so that easily distracted spirits wouldn't catch glimpses of themselves on the way out and decide to stay; the removal of the body from the home through the back door, feet first, to confuse the spirit so it would get lost if it ever tried to return; the zigzag funeral march with the coffin to the countryside grave, the convulsing bodies of the village wailers, who cry with the same intensity at every burial. Mourning is so communal that only the least fortunate and most hated are considered doomed enough to bear it alone.

When we sat down to watch the funeral, the Zoom link did not work. I didn't want to text her daughter during her mother's service to ask for the correct code. *Maybe we were not meant to watch.* Maybe my neighbor did not want us to.

That afternoon, while my neighbor was being buried, some new neighbors, people who'd moved in during the pandemic, blasted loud rap and rock and roll music at the highest possible volume, just as they had nearly every weekend since they arrived. At first, their booming serenade seemed defiant. They were young people who could not go out in one of the world's party capitals. My young neighbors were among those fleeing the virus elsewhere, only to find that it had followed them at an accelerated pace. The pandemic had also eliminated the possibility of our even thinking of walking to their door and introducing ourselves or inviting them to mourn with us by lowering the volume of their music, the blaring celebration of their youth and survival.

As our new neighbors' loud music thumped throughout the

whole block, my mother-in-law and I walked to our front gate and tried to scold them from a distance with our stares.

"Why would they not silence that music for this one day?" my mother-in-law said. "They should be mourning too."

They were indeed mourning, as we would later realize when we noticed the small Black Lives Matter cardboard protest sign on one of their windows. That summer, there was a lot to mourn. We had all watched the May 25 on-camera asphyxiation of George Floyd, his neck crushed beneath the bent knee of Derek Chauvin for nearly nine minutes, as two other officers dug their knees into Floyd's back. Floyd's seemingly unending death had come in the midst of a pandemic that, in the United States, had disproportionately killed Black, Brown, and Indigenous people. A week later, my husband and I, previously afraid to go out among other people, joined weekly protests near our home. In addition to cries for justice for George Floyd and other victims of police and vigilante murder, there were spoken-word recitals, music, drumming, and political hip-hop blasting from cars trailing the crowds. At times, also playing from a car's loudspeaker were the words, and voice, of the then-Miami-based poet and activist Aja Monet, from her poem "#sayhername":

> *I am not here to say look at me how I died*
> *so brutal a death I deserve a name to fit all the horror in*

2

I was twenty when Yusuf K. Hawkins, a sixteen-year-old African American man, was attacked by a mob of about thirty white teenagers armed with baseball bats and then shot to death, on August 23, 1989, in Bensonhurst, Brooklyn. Hawkins had gone to the predominantly white neighborhood to buy a car. In the days and weeks following his death, there were marches, led by the Reverend Al Sharpton and a coalition of civil rights organizations, through the neighborhood where Hawkins was killed.

At the time of Hawkins's murder, I had been in the United States for only eight years. Having spent my childhood living under the ruthless Duvalier dictatorship and being constantly reminded to avoid the wrath of soldiers and henchmen, I was already haunted by stories of beatings, torture, and extrajudicial killings. This was, in part, why I went to a massive protest in downtown Brooklyn a week after the murder. The march, called A Day of Outrage and Mourning, was attended by more than seven thousand people. I took my teenage brothers with me, and I remember fearing—as we marched down Flatbush Avenue, shouting "No justice, no peace"—that one day I might be chanting for them.

We came close on August 9, 1997, when a family friend, Abner Louima, in a case of mistaken identity, was arrested outside a Brooklyn nightclub, then was pummeled with several officers' fists, radios, flashlights, and nightsticks, and sexually assaulted with a wooden broom handle inside a precinct bathroom. Some Black immigrant parents harbor the illusion that if their émigré and US-born children are the politest, the best dressed, and the hardest working in school, they might somehow escape incidents like this. But the myth of the good immigrant as exempt from police assault and murder kept getting shattered around us. By the February 4, 1999, killing of Amadou Diallo, a twenty-three-year-old Guinean, slaughtered on his doorstep by nineteen of the forty-one bullets aimed at him as he reached for his wallet; by the March 16, 2000, shooting of Patrick Dorismond, the twenty-six-year-old son of Haitian immigrants, by undercover officers.

In the Haiti of the nineteen-seventies and early eighties, government detractors were dragged out of their homes, imprisoned, beaten, or killed. Sometimes their bodies were left out in the streets, in the hot sun, for hours or days, to intimidate their neighbors. In New York, the violence was a bit more subtle. When I started riding New York City Transit buses between my family's apartment and the high school I attended, three miles away, I noticed that a muffled radio message from an annoyed bus driver—about someone talking too loudly, or not having the right fare—was all it took to make the police rush in, drag a young Black man off the bus, and beat him into submission on the sidewalk. There were no cell phone cameras back then to record such abuse, and most of us were too terrified to cry "Shame!" or demand a badge number. Besides, many of us had fled our countries to escape this kind of aggression, so we knew how deadly a confrontation with an armed and uniformed figure could be. Still, every now and then fellow travelers would summon their courage and, dodging the swaying baton, or screaming from a distance, would yell some variation of "Stop it! Stop it!"

We marched for all of them, Abner Louima, Amadou Diallo, Patrick Dorismond, and Sean Bell, whose car was shot at fifty times on November 25, 2006, the day of his wedding, and sixty-six-year-old Eleanor Bumpurs, who, thirteen years before Abner's assault, was killed with a twelve-gauge police shotgun inside her own apartment. We carried signs and chanted "No justice, no peace!" and "Whose streets? Our streets!" even while fearing that this would never be true. Just as they did in the places we came from, the streets belonged to the people with the uniforms and the guns, so much so that a man using a counterfeit twenty-dollar bill in a store ends up being choked to death beneath a police officer's knee.

3

In June 2015, nearly a year after eighteen-year-old Michael Brown was killed by police officer Darren Wilson in Ferguson, Missouri, and soon after Dylann Roof, a white supremacist, walked into Emanuel African Methodist Episcopal Church in Charleston, South Carolina, during evening Bible study and murdered nine people, I walked the long rectangular room at New York's Museum of Modern Art where Jacob Lawrence's *Migration Series* was on display. I had seen many of the paintings before, in books and magazines, but never in person. I'd somehow expected them to be as colossal as their subject, the fifty-five-year-plus mass migration of more than six million African Americans from the rural South to urban centers in the northern United States.

Each of the sixty spare and, at times, appropriately stark tempera paintings in the series measures twelve by eighteen inches and is underscored by a descriptive caption written by the artist, whose parents moved from Virginia and South Carolina to New Jersey, where he was born. The size of the paintings quickly became inconsequential as I moved from panel to panel, the first one showing a crowd of people crammed into a train station and filing toward ticket windows marked Chicago, New York, St. Louis, and the last panel returning us to yet another railroad station, showing that in spite of dangerous and unhealthy working conditions and race riots in the North, the migrants "kept coming."

At the end of a week when nine men and women had been brutally assassinated by a white supremacist in Charleston, South Carolina, and the possibility of two hundred thousand Haitians and Dominicans of Haitian descent being expelled from the Dominican Republic suddenly became very real, I longed to be in the presence of Lawrence's migrants and survivors. I was yearning for their witness and fellowship, to borrow language from some of the churches that ended up being lifelines for the Great Migration's new arrivals. But what kept me glued to these silhouettes is how beautifully and heartbreakingly Lawrence captured Black bodies in motion, in transit, in danger, and in pain. The bowed heads of the hungry and the curved backs of mourners helped the Great Migration to gain and keep its momentum, along with the promise of less abject poverty and more opportunities in the North.

Human beings have been migrating since the beginning of time. We have always traveled from place to place looking for better prospects, where they exist. We are not always welcomed, especially if we are viewed as different and dangerous, or if we end up, as Toni Morrison described in her Nobel lecture, on the edges of towns that cannot bear our company. The nine men and women who were senselessly murdered by a young white supremacist at Emanuel African Methodist Episcopal Church on June 17, 2015, were home. They were in their own country, among family and friends, and they believed themselves to be in the presence of God. And yet before they were massacred, they were subjected to a variation of the same detestable vitriol that unwanted immigrants everywhere face: "You're taking over our country, and you have to go."

In the hateful manifesto posted on his website, the killer, Dylann Roof, also wrote, "As an American we are taught to accept living in the melting pot, and black and other minorities have just as much right to be here as we do, since we are all immigrants. But Europe is the homeland of White people, and in many ways the situation is even worse there." I wonder if he had in mind Europe's most recent migrants, especially those who'd drowned by the thousands in the waters of the Mediterranean Sea while fleeing oppression and wars in sub-Saharan and northern

Africa and the Middle East. Or maybe he was thinking of all those nonwhite people who are European citizens, though not by his standards. This white supremacist charged himself with deciding who can stay and who can go, and the only uncontestable way he knew to carry out his venomous decree was to kill.

In *The Warmth of Other Suns*, the Pulitzer Prize–winning journalist Isabel Wilkerson writes that, during the Great Migration, "The people did not cross the turnstiles of customs at Ellis Island. They were already citizens. But where they came from, they were not treated as such." Nearly every migrant Wilkerson interviewed justifiably resisted being called an immigrant. "The idea conjured up the deepest pains of centuries of rejection by their own country," she writes.

Tragically, we do not always get the final say on how our Black bodies are labeled. Those fleeing the South during the Great Migration were sometimes referred to not only as immigrants but as refugees, just as the US citizens who were internally displaced by Hurricane Katrina in the summer of 2005 were given that label after the storm. Dominicans of Haitian descent also thought themselves to be at home in the Dominican Republic. The Dominican constitution grants citizenship to all those who are born in the country, unless they are the children of people "in transit." Dominicans of Haitian descent whose families have lived in the country for generations are still considered to be in transit. Black bodies, living with "certain uncertainty," to use Frantz Fanon's words, can be in transit, it seems, for several generations.

White supremacists such as Dylann Roof like to speak of Black bodies as though they are dangerous weapons. Xenophobes often speak of migrants and immigrants as though they are an invasion force, or something akin to biological warfare. Wallace Best, a religion and Great Migration scholar, writes that "a black body in motion is never without consequence. It is always a signifier of something, scripted and coded. And for the most part, throughout our history black bodies in motion have been deemed a threat." Along with their vivid colors and sharp symmetrical shapes, Jacob Lawrence's paintings conjure the hypervigilance required to live and love, work and play, travel and pray in a Black body.

A year later, I was in Haiti, on the southernmost border between Haiti and the Dominican Republic, where hundreds of Haitian refugees either had been deported or had been driven out of the Dominican Republic by intimidation or threats. Many of these men, women, and children had very little warning that they were going to be picked up or chased away, and most of them had fled with nothing but the clothes on their backs.

It was a bright sunny day, but the air was so thick with dust that as some friends and I walked through the makeshift resettlement camps on the Haitian side of the border, in a place called Pak Kado, it felt as though we, along with the residents of the camps, were floating through clouds. Around us were lean-tos made of cardboard boxes and sheets. Dust-covered children walked around looking dazed even while they were playing with pebbles that stood in for marbles, or flying plastic bags as kites. Elderly people stood on the edge of food and clothes distribution lines, some too weak to wade into the crowd. Later the elderly, pregnant women, and people with disabilities would be given special consideration by the priest and nuns who were distributing the only food available to the camp dwellers, but the food would always run out before they could get to everyone.

A few days after leaving Haiti and returning to the United States, I read a Michael Brown anniversary opinion piece in the *Washington Post* written by Raha Jorjani, an immigration attorney and law professor. In her essay, Jorjani argues that African Americans living in the United States could easily qualify as refugees. Citing many recent cases of police brutality and killings of unarmed Black men, women, and children, she wrote:

> *Suppose a client walked into my office and told me that police officers in his country had choked a man to death over a petty crime. Suppose he said police fatally shot another man in the back as he ran away. That they arrested a woman during a traffic stop and placed her in jail, where she died three days later. That a 12-year-old boy in his country was shot and killed by the police as he played in the park.*
>
> *Suppose he told me that all of those victims were from the same ethnic community—a community whose members fear being harmed, tortured or killed by police or prison guards. And that this is true in cities and towns across his nation. At that point, as an immigration lawyer, I'd tell him he had a strong claim for asylum protection under U.S. law.*

Having visited many refugee and displacement camps, I initially thought this label hyperbolic especially when assigned to citizens of one of the richest countries in the world, and on a singular basis, that they are Black. Still, compared to the relative wealth of the rest of the society, perhaps a particular falling-apart Brooklyn public housing project where a childhood friend used to live could have easily been considered a kind of refugee camp, occupying one of the most economically disadvantaged parts of town and providing only the most basic necessities. The nearby dilapidating school easily could have been on the edge of that refugee settlement. Were we all members of an in-transit group?

Parents are often too nervous to broach difficult subjects with their children. Love. Sex. Death. Race. But sometimes we're forced to have these conversations early. Too early. A broken heart might lead to questions we'd rather not answer, as might an inappropriate gesture, the death of a loved one, or the murder of a stranger. Each time a young Black person is killed by a police officer or by a vigilante civilian, I ask myself if the time has come for me to write to my daughters a letter about Abner Louima and the long list of nonsurvivors who have come after him. *By the time you read this . . .*

"What kind of mother/ing is it if one must always be prepared with knowledge of the possibility of the violent and quotidian death of one's child?" ponders Christina Sharpe in *In the Wake*. I don't want my daughters to grow up terrified of the country and the world they live in, but is it irresponsible of me not to at least alert them to the potentially life-altering, or even life-ending, horrors they might face as young Black women who might, even though they were born in the United States, possibly classify for refugee status here?

The night President Barack Obama was first elected (Would he too qualify for refugee status?) my older daughter, Mira, was three years old and I was in the last weeks of my pregnancy with her sister Leila. When President Obama was inaugurated for the first time, I was cradling both girls in my arms.

To think, I remember telling my husband, our daughters in their early years will never know a world in which the president of this country has not been Black. Indeed, as we watched President Obama's inaugural speech, Mira was shocked that no woman had been president of the United States. The world ahead for my girls seemed, at least that day, full of greater possibilities than that of the generations that had preceded them, both as migrants and hosts. However, it quickly became clear that this one man was not going to take us into a postracial promised land. Donald Trump's "birther" claims and the bigoted commentaries and jokes by both elected officials and ordinary folk never seemed to stop. Initially one of the most consistent attacks against Obama was that he was not really American.

Like Barack Obama's father, many of us had come to America from somewhere else and needed to have two different talks with our Black offspring: one about why we're here, and the other one about why it's not always a promised land for people who look like us.

In his own version of "the Talk," James Baldwin wrote to his nephew James in "My Dungeon Shook": "You were born into a society which spelled out with brutal clarity, and in as many ways as possible, that you were a worthless human being."

That same letter could have been written to a long roster of dead young men and women, including Michael Brown. It's sad to imagine what these young people's letters from their loved ones would have said. *By the time you read this . . .* Would their favorite uncle have notified them that they could qualify for refugee status within their own country? Would their mother or father, grandmother or grandfather have warned them to not walk, stroll, or jog in certain white majority neighborhoods, to, impossibly, avoid police officers, to never play in a public park, to stay away from neighborhood watchmen, to never go to a neighbor's house and, even if they were in danger, seek help there?

I am still drafting a "My Dungeon Shook" letter to my daughters in a pocket-size notebook.

By time you read this, will this too have passed?

To my evolving draft of this letter, I often add snippets of Baldwin's letter.

"I tell you this because I love you, and please don't you ever forget it," Baldwin reminded his James. "Know whence you came.

If you know whence you came, there is really no limit to where you can go."

So, as a living letter, my husband and I took my daughters to the Haitian Dominican border between Malpasse and Jimaní, a border redrawn by Americans in 1936. In 1916, the United States invaded the Dominican Republic for the first time, annexing Haiti and the Dominican Republic for eight years, between 1916 and 1924. The occupation of the Dominican Republic, like the 1915–1934 occupation of Haiti, was motivated by regional and commercial interests.

"In the Dominican Republic, American multinationals laid out vast new sugar plantations, which needed more workers than Santo Domingo could provide," Michele Wucker writes in *Why the Cocks Fight: Dominicans, Haitians, and the Struggle for Hispaniola*. "Haiti, with the same population but half the land, was a natural source, so the companies moved thousands of people across the border, establishing a steady flow from west to east."

At the Jimaní-Malpasse border, there was still a flow of laborers dragging empty wheelbarrows past heavily armed guards through a dusty gate into the Dominican Republic, then returning loaded with merchandise. With the court ruling allowing for the expulsion of Haitian residents of the Dominican Republic and Dominicans of Haitian descent, there was also another kind of flow. At a nearby school and church on the Haitian side of the border, we met dozens of people who told us how they were picked up by police and soldiers in the Dominican Republic, put in the back of pickup trucks, and dropped at the border. Some were Haitian-born, but many were Dominican-born, especially the children. Many had cards saying that they had registered for a "regularization" program, which was supposed to guarantee them some protection, but did not.

At the school, my daughters helped to comfort children who had been rejected by a country they considered their own, and were waiting to see whether their parents' and grandparents' homeland would accept them.

"You think your pain and your heartbreak are unprecedented in the history of the world, but then you read," James Baldwin wrote.

By the time you read this . . .

Chronicles of a Death Foretold

Sè Laura, a forty-three-year-old self-proclaimed prophetess, spent months trying to tell Haitian president Jovenel Moïse that he was going to die. She wrote him letters that she unsuccessfully tried to deliver to him at the National Palace in Port-au-Prince. She traveled to his hometown in the northeast of the country and tried to meet with his son at their banana plantation. She even attended his mother-in-law's funeral, passing herself off as a well-wisher. When they finally came face-to-face after the service, she asked if she could meet with him alone so she could deliver her message privately. He shrugged her off and moved on to the next person. She had no choice, she said, but to take her message to the airways, via some of Haiti's most popular radio stations: President Jovenel Moïse would die while he was in office. Six months later, he was assassinated.

During the final moments of his life, the fifty-three-year-old Moïse was as abandoned and unprotected as Haiti's most vulnerable citizens. His body and face riddled with at least twelve bullets—including one that gouged his left eye—he was killed in the early morning hours of July 7, 2021, in the bedroom of his home on a narrow street in the hills above Port-au-Prince. Haitian government and police officials immediately reported that he was killed by a band of foreign mercenaries, among them two Haitian Americans and twenty-six Colombian nationals, who the authorities claimed were recruited by a sixty-two-year-old Florida-based Haitian pastor, Christian Emmanuel Sanon, who was plotting to replace Moïse as president, with help from CTU, a Miami-area security firm owned by Venezuelan and Colombian émigrés. According to cell phone video recordings taken by Moïse's neighbors, the assailants gained access to Moïse's residence by declaring that they were part of a United States Drug Enforcement Agency operation. No casualties were reported among the presidential guard or any other security agents whom one would expect to defend the premises. Though two of the presidential couple's grown children were also in the home, Moïse's wife, Martine, was the only other person wounded in the attack. (She was shot in her right arm.) Martine Moïse was taken to a local hospital by a police official, who arrived after the assailants left, and then she was medevacked to Miami's Ryder Trauma Center.

Jovenel Moïse came to power after a two-round election cycle, in 2015 and 2016, with the lowest turnout in Haiti's brief history of postdictatorship elections. In a country of eleven million people, he received around six hundred thousand votes. Moïse was unknown to most Haitians until he was handpicked by his predecessor, Michel Martelly, a konpa singer known as Sweet Micky, who came to power, in 2011, through another set of contested elections. Moïse at the time was a banana exporter (with the nickname Nèg Bannann, or Banana Man), and he was sold as a self-made, successful rural entrepreneur from outside of Haiti's political class. In fact, Agritans, Moïse's banana company, had received millions of dollars from Martelly's government—funds that, according to Haiti's Superior Court of Auditors and Administrative Disputes, were among those pilfered from Venezuela's Petrocaribe oil program, through which the Haitian government bought oil from Venezuela, paid 60 percent of the purchase price within ninety days, then deferred the rest of the debt, at a 1 percent interest rate, over twenty-five years. This debt to Venezuela grew to $2.3 billion. In early 2024, the debt was settled for $500 million.

On July 6, 2018, I was in Haiti when Moïse's government announced that it was raising the price of gasoline, diesel, and kerosene. Nationwide demonstrations demanding his resignation followed, and lasted for months. In response, Moïse vowed to complete his contested term, reform the country's constitution, and hold the next legislative and presidential elections. During Moïse's time in office, government-connected gangs carried out thirteen massacres in poor opposition neighborhoods. The International Human Rights Clinic at Harvard Law School and the Haitian Observatory for Crimes Against Humanity studied three of these thirteen massacres that they defined as crimes against humanity.

Two days before his assassination, Moïse named Ariel Henry, a neurosurgeon and former interior minister, as his seventh prime minister. Soon after he was sworn into office on July 20, 2021, phone records revealed that Henry had spoken to one of the assassination's lead suspects between 4:03 a.m. and 4:20 a.m. on July 7, around three hours after the president was killed. That suspect, Joseph Felix Badio, a former Ministry of Justice Anti-Corruption Unit employee, who had been fired for possible corruption, happened to be near the president's home at the time he'd allegedly called Henry. Henry has said that he does not remember the call. Badio was arrested more than two years later, in October 2023.

After Moïse's assassination, I thought a lot about Gabriel García Márquez's *Chronicle of a Death Foretold*. In the novella, twin brothers Pedro and Pablo Vicario announce to everyone who will listen that they will kill Santiago Nassar for deflowering their sister, who's forced to return home in shame on her wedding night. Though many people know what's about to happen, no one tries to save Santiago Nassar. Even the investigative judge probing Santiago Nassar's murder is perplexed that "life should make use of so many coincidences forbidden literature, so that there should be the untrammeled fulfillment of a death so clearly foretold."

According to the *Miami Herald*, Moïse kept a diary of sorts, a notebook in which he wrote about "a tentative coup d'état and the need to track down the full name of a certain pastor named Sanon, who was rumored to have presidential aspirations." A friend of Moïse's, a former senator named Jacques Sauveur Jean, told a Haitian radio broadcaster that the night before he died, Moïse told him on the phone that he knew millions had been raised to finance a plot to assassinate him. Yet, he did not seem worried.

"I used to ask the president, if he had information about threats, why didn't he go public?" Jean told *Miami Herald* reporter Jacqueline Charles. "He would say, I'm going to get them. He thought he had enough collaborators to arrest all of them, and they wouldn't get a chance to kill him."

I was reading Márquez's novella once again when my mother-in-law introduced me, via WhatsApp and YouTube, to the fortune-telling talents of Sè Laura, who was apparently one of many who had foreseen, and foretold, Moïse's death. After Moïse's assassination, Sè Laura became a kind of macabre sensation in my mother-in-law's older, and mostly female, evangelical circle. Sè Laura was stopped on the streets of Port-au-Prince and her comments were streamed live on Facebook. She was reinvited to some of the radio programs where she'd predicted Moïse's death, and was interviewed in greater detail.

Sè Laura was from Belladère, in the Central Department of the country, she said. Her father had eighteen children, four with her mother. One brother died in childhood and two sisters were living in the United States and Canada. She has four children of her own. She has been a Christian for twenty-two years, though she doesn't attend any particular church. One of her frequent interviewers, Pierre Richard Guillaume, the host of *Blocus,* a YouTube program focused on spirituality and the occult, told her when she appeared on *Blocus* in mid-August 2021 that he'd heard she was arrested as part of the investigation into the president's death. Sè Laura was rumored to be the cousin of one of the accused, a judge who'd allegedly signed an arrest warrant for the president that some of the Colombian mercenaries said they thought they were carrying out the night of the assassination. Sè Laura denied knowing the judge, or that they were related. She has not been arrested.

Sè Laura was not the only prophet or prophetess to emerge before and after Moïse's death. "Prophets have been sprouting like mushrooms in Haiti," Guilluame told her during their August 2021 interview. Some of the other prophets claimed that Moïse's death would make way for them to be crowned kings or queens of a new Haiti, and that many of the country's trials and tribulations would be a stepping stone for Haiti's future glory, when the country would be turned into a theocratic Christian paradise. Whether they were living in Haiti or the Haitian diaspora, many of the prophets and prophetesses echoed foreign evangelicals, including the former Republican presidential candidate Pat Robertson, who after the January 12, 2010, earthquake said that Haiti was cursed because the country's revolution was launched at an August 14, 1791, Vodou ceremony in the north of Haiti at Bois Caïman. Sé Laura, however, prophesied that she would become Haiti's next president, and that God himself would hand her the job as there would never be another election held in Haiti again.

Three months to the day after Jovenel Moïse's assassination, on October 7, 2021, his brother, Gabriel Moïse, was a guest on a much-listened-to midmorning news-and-commentary-as-entertainment radio program called *Matin débat*, which was one of the first places that Sè Laura had announced the president's imminent death. On *Matin débat*, the hosts, including the show's famous anchor, Louko Désir, ring a bell each time they make or someone they are interviewing makes what they consider an interesting point. The morning Gabriel Moïse was on the show, the bell was rung a lot. Gabriel Moïse told Louko Désir that he knew his brother would be assassinated, though perhaps not while in office. Everyone knew, Gabriel Moïse said, that the president had some extremely powerful enemies, including some wealthy oligarchs, who for decades had been benefiting from extremely lucrative and questionable government contracts, which Moïse had publicly challenged, and in some cases tried to take away.

"I know that a lot of people he spoke about would not have tolerated what he said," Gabriel Moïse told Louko Désir on the air. "There are things that if you say to someone just between the two of you, it stays between you two, but as soon as you say it publicly, you will die. Jovenel Moïse had no allies," his brother added.

The police investigation concurred.

"A paranoid president who trusted no one, Moïse ran his own camera surveillance system and was a man without friends," Jacqueline Charles and Jay Weaver wrote in the *Miami Herald*, on September 20, 2021, after reviewing a detailed report on the assassination investigation. As his killers were encroaching in the early morning hours of July 7, Moïse made several telephone calls seeking help from the police chief and the inspector general, as well a high-level security official, Jean Laguel Civil, who, according to the police report, had paid security agents to stand down that night. Usually there are between thirty and fifty security personnel posted at the president's residence. The night Moïse was assassinated, there were fewer than ten. The head of the General Security Unit of the National Palace, Dimitri Hérard, who had been credited by Moïse with saving him from an alleged assassination attempt in February 2021, was accused of having helped plan the assassination, and providing guns and ammunition to the Colombian mercenaries. Hérard also happened to be under investigation by US law enforcement officials for arms trafficking. The Haitian Americans—James Solages, Joseph Vincent, and Christian Emmanuel Sanon, who saw himself as a potential replacement for Moïse—were later transferred to the United States, where they were charged with conspiring to commit murder or kidnapping outside the United States. Mario Palacios Palacios, a former Colombian military officer, was arrested in Kingston, Jamaica, and was taken into FBI custody during a layover in Panama as he was being returned to Colombia. In mid-November 2021, another suspect, Samir Handal, a sixty-three-year-old Haitian businessman who'd spent time with Christian Emmanuel Sanon before the assassination, was arrested, through an Interpol request, in Turkey then released. Another suspect, a former Haitian senator named John Joël Joseph, was arrested in Jamaica, where he had been hiding for months. In February 2023, four US-based suspects were taken into custody, including Antonio Intriago and Arcángel Pretel Ortiz, the owners of CTU, the Miami security firm, and the Florida-based financiers Walter Veintemilla and Frederick J. Bergmann. In 2023, Rodolphe Jaar, a Haitian Chilean businessman and convicted drug trafficker turned Drug Enforcement Administration informant, and Germán Alejandro Rivera García, a retired Colombian colonel, along with Bergmann,

García, Vincent, Palacios Palacios, and John Joël Joseph, pleaded guilty to conspiracy to kidnap, murder, and provide material support for the assassination.

In February 2024, a Haitian judge, Walther Wesser Voltaire, indicted fifty individuals in the president's assassination, including his former police chief, Léon Charles, his former prime minister, Claude Joseph, and his wife, Martine Moïse, whom the judge accused of being complicit in his assassination in part because she wanted to replace him.

"This is Julius Caesar with a twist even Shakespeare didn't think of," commented a friend.

Moïse, too, had occasionally made statements that indicated he might have foreseen his own death. On several occasions, including at a town hall at the National Palace in September 2020, he said that whenever Haitian presidents try to change the status quo, "Either they kill you, and they kill you in many different ways. They demonize you. They assassinate your character. They eliminate you, shoot you, or send you into exile."

During a precarnival speech in Jacmel, in February 2021, Moïse railed against a "system" that he said was sucking the country dry. This system, he emphasized, goes back centuries, to when Africans were abducted from the continent and enslaved on the island. Jean Jacques Dessalines, one of Haiti's founding fathers, and the first Black head of state in the Americas, had fought against this system, Moïse said, beating the French on November 18, 1803, at the Battle of Vertières, the final campaign in a twelve-year war for independence. Dessalines was assassinated three years later. By invoking both Africa and Dessalines's assassination, Moïse was alluding to the fact that Dessalines's lighter-skinned political rivals had conspired to kill him. The system, he implied, was now being run by the country's lighter-hued oligarchs, whom he referred to as "a category of people who say that they are people and that we are not.

"After you killed Dessalines, you've killed presidents. You've assassinated presidents. You've exiled presidents. You've imprisoned presidents. Don't forget there's one last president who is stuck in your throats," he said, referring to himself.

He ended up being right about his killers' inability to obliterate him. He was even stuck in international journalists' throats. After his assassination, few articles were ever written or reported about Haiti without mentioning him and how the country continued to spiral in the months and years since his death.

Between July and September 2021, Martine Moïse gave a series of interviews to foreign journalists. In late July, she described to Frances Robles of the *New York Times* being awakened by gunfire in the early morning hours of July 7, then running to her adult children's bedrooms to tell them to hide, with their dog, in a bathroom. When she returned to her husband's side, she found him calling for help. He reached Civil and Hérard by phone. They said they were coming to his rescue but never showed up. As the assassins moved in, her husband told her to lie down on the floor, his final words to her. The mercenaries then burst through the door. Their bullets struck her first, in her right arm. As she lay on the ground, she saw only her husband's killers' boots.

"Then I closed my eyes, and I didn't see anything else," she told Robles.

The Spanish-speaking assassins were talking to someone on the phone as they searched for a document, which they eventually found. Martine Moïse said she did not know what kind of document it was, but in December 2021, the *New York Times* reported that it was a list of "powerful politicians and businesspeople involved in Haiti's drug trade," a list that the president intended to hand over to US government officials. On the list apparently were former president Martelly's brother-in-law and other wealthy businesspeople. On the way out the door, after killing her husband, one of the assassins waved a flashlight in her eyes, possibly to see if she was dead. She managed to convincingly appear dead, Martine Moïse said.

In her interview with CNN reporter Matt Rivers, which aired on August 3, 2021, Martine Moïse said that her husband was still alive, and unhurt, after the dozen or so assassins burst into their bedroom looking for the document in question. They shot her husband only after verifying with the person on the phone that it was him.

On August 14, 2021, a 7.2 magnitude earthquake struck Haiti's southern peninsula and killed more than twenty-two hundred people. The earthquake destroyed schools, churches, health facilities, and thousands of homes, including, we learned while my mother-in-law was in Miami, her home in Gros Marin, which had been repaired after Hurricane Matthew in 2016. A tropical storm, Grace, battered the same area soon after. In early October 2021, Martine Moïse traveled to several towns in the earthquake- and hurricane-ravaged southern peninsula, where she was greeted by crowds chanting, "Yo tiye Papa. N a p vote Manman." They killed our father. We'll vote for our mother.

Whether they will vote for this particular mother remains to be seen. The prophetess Sè Laura told *Blocus*'s Pierre Richard Guillaume that if she, Laura, does not become president of Haiti, she will die. (As of this writing, she is still alive and not the president of Haiti. Nearly three years after Moïse's assassination, there are no elected officials in the country.)

On July 23, 2021, Jovenel Moïse's funeral was held at his family's compound, where his flag-draped coffin rested on the side of a crowded stage with four young men in military dress uniforms standing guard. As far as we know, Sè Laura was not present at that funeral. A large billboard of Moïse's face loomed over both his family members and the dignitaries on the stage, as well as his supporters in the crowd below. Sounds of gunfire rang out outside, and the smell of tear gas and smoke drifted into the compound, forcing the US delegation to depart early, and hurriedly.

Her right arm in a cast, Martine Moïse was dressed in a caped black dress with a red rose corsage pinned to her lapel. She covered her recently cropped hair with a wide-brimmed black hat, and removed a black face mask with her husband's photo affixed to it in order to deliver her bilingual (French, then Creole) eulogy. She recalled meeting her husband as a young man and finding him "brilliant, inventive, creative, passionate, and determined."

"This young man charmed me and won my heart," she said. She too railed against the system. "They assassinated President Jovenel, but they cannot assassinate his vision. They cannot assassinate his ideas. They cannot assassinate his dreams for his country. We lost a battle but not the war. The fight is not over. The vultures are still running the streets with their claws and hooks, still bloody, they are still in search of prey. They are not even hiding. They are here, watching us, listening to us, hoping to frighten us. Their thirst for blood has not yet been quenched."

Wozo, Not Mawozo

By mid-October 2021, Haiti was in the news regularly again, this time as a result of the kidnapping of seventeen missionaries by a heavily armed gang called 400 Mawozo, notorious for mass kidnappings of locals and foreigners. The missionaries included five men, seven women, and five children. Sixteen were from the United States, and one from Canada. The missionaries were among the 782 people who'd been reported kidnapped that year, earning Haiti a new moniker in the international press: the country with the world's highest kidnapping rate per capita. 400 Mawozo demanded $17 million for the missionaries' release, and their leader, Wilson Joseph, also known as Lanmò san jou (Death Without Warning/Death Without Days), threatened to kill them if he didn't receive the full ransom.

Before abducting these seventeen Mennonites and Anabaptists from the Ohio-based Christian Aid Ministries, 400 Mawozo had previously held transport buses full of people, and five French Catholic priests and two nuns, for ransom. The group operated out of Croix-des-Bouquets, a commune about eight miles northeast of Port-au-Prince. Home to around half a million people,

Croix-des-Bouquets is known for its signature steel metal art, or metal *dekoupe*: silhouetted images carved out of recycled oil drums. Metal *dekoupe* grew from the work of a local blacksmith named Georges Liautaud, who, in the 1940s, carved wrought iron wreaths and cut metal crosses for funerals. Liautaud's pieces were seen in local cemeteries by the American DeWitt Peters, co-founder with Haitian artists and intellectuals such as Maurice Borno and Albert Mangonès of Haiti's famous Centre d'Art, where Liautaud and others were encouraged to expand their daily labor into art.

At a square near Croix-des-Bouquets' Metal Arts District, whose center is the Village Artistique de Noailles, the artist friend who'd taken me there had said that Georges Liautaud's crosses and metal *dekoupe* art was wozo.

"Most Haitians are wozo," he'd added.

Wozo—*roseau* in French—is an irrepressible reed that grows in marshlands and riverbeds despite impossible conditions. No matter what happens to wozo, it springs back. If the wind blows it over, it rises again. If a flood drowns it, it sinks into the earth for a while, then shoots up again. If you burn and raze it in the dirt, it will reemerge even stronger.

There's a saying that's often sung, either as the chorus of other songs—as in "Wozo" by the singer Belo—or as a short rhyme.

> Nou se wozo.
> Menm si nou pliye,
> nou pap kase.

> We are wozo.
> Even if we bend,
> we will not break.

I know there's some hyperbolic mythology in all of this. All-powerful plants are like the almighty saints, saviors, and warriors we aspire to emulate but would rather not be forced to. It's like being constantly called resilient because people think you're able to suffer much more than others. Still, better that we are wozo than prey, my artist friend had said. Better that we are wozo than Mawozo, he added recently as we recalled our visits to Croix-des-Bouquets, me from Miami and him from the outskirts of Port-au-Prince, in Carrefour.

Four days before they kidnapped the missionaries, the 400 Mawozo gang attacked the Village Artistique de Noailles. Over fifty years old, the village is home to close to four hundred artists and eighty ateliers, as well as four well-frequented *peristil*, landmark Vodou temples. During a shoot-out with police, 400 Mawozo invaded the area and opened fire on the artists' shops and residences, killing a well-known sculptor, Anderson Belony. I had been to the village many times, strolling through the compound lined with art shops filled with flat metal sculptures of different shapes and sizes, depicting trees, flowers, butterflies, birds, lizards, snakes, suns, moons, stars, fish, crosses, mermaids, and *vèvès*, drawings of Vodou deities, including that of Lasirèn, the goddess of the sea. Some of the shops' walls were also covered with Bible verses carved in metal, as well as tourist bait phrases such as "Dream Big," "Coffee Is Always a Good Idea," "Always Kiss Me Good Night." Some shops had three-dimensional mixed-media sculptures with pots and pans, car parts, mirrors, dolls, and musical instruments attached to the metal *dekoupe*. You could buy furniture in some workshops: a few chairs or an entire dining room set. In the yards and alleys, if you were lucky, you could spot an artist stenciling or drawing an image or pattern right before it was chiseled, polished, varnished, and sometimes coated in bright colors.

I thought 400 Mawozo had named themselves after the wozo, adding the Kreyòl word *ma* (meaning "the rest" or "what's left") as a prefix to suggest that they were not just wozo but the roots of the wozo, the source of the plant's ceaseless regeneration. But after 400 Mawozo kidnapped the seventeen missionaries and became known around the world, I was reminded by my artist friend of the actual meaning of the idiomatic word. A *mawozo* is a man who lacks panache, who doesn't know how to speak to or woo women, a kind of Cyrano de Bergerac. The gang's name, 400 Mawozo, is self-mocking, a "fawouch," my friend said. The American press translated 400 Mawozo as 400 good-for-nothings, 400 simpletons or 400 inexperienced men (the *Washington Post*), and, my personal favorite, 400 idiots (Reuters).

Reuters has reported that 400 Mawozo started out as small-time thieves. They had initially named themselves Texas, perhaps due to the Lone Star State's outlaw image. They stole livestock and motorcycles, and commandeered public transportation buses and containers heading to and from the Dominican border. One of the origin stories I heard on a Montreal-based Haitian YouTubers' commentary feed is that Wilson Joseph started his first neighborhood gang as a teenager. Apparently, he did so after seeing a spaghetti vendor slap his destitute mother for not paying an accumulated debt for the cooked spaghetti breakfast she'd bought on credit every morning to feed him. This might be, in part, why Joseph, like many of the other gang leaders who grew up in the *geto*, the poor areas they occupy, claim that they are also helping the poor. (*N ap fè sosyal.*)

As the seventeen missionaries entered their third week in captivity, a criminal complaint filed by the FBI was unsealed, revealing that three Florida residents had been smuggling weapons to 400 Mawozo. The Floridians—Eliande Tunis, Jocelyn Dor, and Walder St. Louis—received the gang's wish list via WhatsApp messages, bought the weapons from licensed arms dealers and pawnshops all over Florida, then shipped them, via a cargo company, in the large blue barrels that are as present as furniture in some working-class Haitian American homes. While Dor and St. Louis did most of the weapons and ammunition shopping, the shipping and communication were done by Tunis, a naturalized US citizen in her early forties, who described herself as the "queen" of 400 Mawozo. According to the FBI complaint, Tunis would wrap the guns in garbage bags and used clothes, adding some Gatorade in the blue barrel for good measure. In her What'sApp correspondence and voice notes with Joseph and another 400 Mawozo leader, Joly "Yonyon" Germine, who was coleading the gang inside a Haitian jail but has since been extradited to the United States, Tunis wrote, "You know we are 400 Mawozo. . . . We are snakes. We slither to get where we are going. They would be shocked to see Mawozo invade Miami."

In early 2024, Germine, Tunis, Dor, and St. Louis pleaded guilty to smuggling and money laundering charges.

It's rare to get detailed public accounts of what it's like to be kidnapped and held for ransom by a group like 400 Mawozo. Father Michel Briand, one of the French priests kidnapped in April 2021 and held for nineteen days, told *New York Times* reporters Maria Abi-Habib and Constant Méheut that he and his group were driving through Croix-des-Bouquets when they were stopped by armed men who forced their way into their car, shoved their driver aside, and drove them all to a rural area. During their first few days in captivity, they slept outside, the priest said, under a tree, on pieces of cardboard. They were then moved to several abandoned homes and finally to one that was like a windowless prison cell. They were fed once a day until the final days, when they were given no food. Father Briand's account was echoed by the Reverend Jean-Nicaisse Milien, who told Associated Press correspondent Dánica Coto in November 2021 that the group was kept blindfolded and "we did our necessities on the ground."

During their last week with the kidnappers, Milien and the others were no longer fed the one daily meal of rice, bread, and Coca-Cola and were given very little water. While they were en route to yet another location, the gang members told them: "Here, we don't have any food, any hospital, any house. We don't have anything, but we have a cemetery." Wilson Joseph offered his version to Guerrier Henri, the host of Radio Mega's *Boukante lapawòl* (Trading Speech), which, like Louko Désir's *Matin débat*, is also a kind of news-and-commentary-as-entertainment show.

"I don't have a hospital or an orphanage in my house, and I don't owe anyone food anymore," Joseph told Guerrier when he was asked, nine days after they were abducted, whether he was still feeding his clergy captives.

These priests and nuns were not the only members of the cloth who'd been kidnapped that year. In April 2021, while their evening service was live-streamed on Facebook, gunmen burst into the Seventh-day Adventist Gospel Kreyòl Ministry Church in Carrefour. They kidnapped the pastor, the church pianist, and two others. In late September, a sixty-year-old deacon, Sylner Lafaille, was killed by an armed group. His wife, Marie Marthe Laurent Lafaille, was abducted as they entered the First Baptist Church of Port-au-Prince. On October 3, seventy-nine-year-old Jean Pierre Ferrer Michel, a US citizen and pastor of the Jesus Center church, was kidnapped by armed men dressed in police uniforms before a Sunday-morning service. He was held for nearly a month.

Wilson Joseph had told Henri on *Boukante lapawòl* that he saw the French priests and nuns as representative of France's sins against Haiti: enslavement, colonization, and "the Ransom" of $150 million that Haiti was forced to pay France for this independence.

"They are the reason Haiti is the way it is today," he added.

The year before, Christian Aid Ministries had settled with Haitian sexual victims for $420,000. These victims had sued the organization after Jeriah Mast, one of their employees, confessed to having molested thirty boys, over fifteen years, while he was working with the organization in Haiti. Two managers had been aware of the abuse for years but did nothing. Mast was serving a nine-year term for molesting minors in Ohio when the missionaries were kidnapped.

The spike in kidnappings of priests, nuns, and pastors reconfigured how segments of the Protestant church worshipped in Haiti. Protestants had been largely apolitical, except during the presidency of Jovenel Moïse. In the summer of 2020, pastors and their flocks collected thousands of signatures in petitions and took to the streets when Moïse's government proposed changing Haiti's penal code to legalize abortion, lower the legal age for consensual sex to fifteen, and make it illegal for clergy to refuse to perform same-sex weddings. After the clergy kidnappings, however, some pastors began to think of new ways to protect themselves and their congregations. The most notable case is that of Jesus Christ Full Gospel Church pastor Job Antoine in Port-au-Prince. Citing Luke 22:36—"Jesus said to them . . . if you don't have a sword, sell your cloak and buy one"—Antoine encouraged his congregants to purchase machetes, which they waved in the air during his sermons.

"Those of us in the Protestant church in this country were taught not to avenge ourselves," Antoine preached. "Vengeance is mine, says the Lord. Thou shall not kill. If anyone slaps you on one cheek, turn the other cheek. That's what we have been taught, right? . . . Contrary to what we have been taught and what we learned in Bible school, we can't stand by and let a man gut us and spill our shit. We'll spill his shit first. Amen?"

The following Sunday, Jesus Christ Full Gospel Church senior pastor Jean Paul Davius, himself formerly kidnapped, quoted the Latin adage *Si vis pacem, para bellum*. "Those who want peace must prepare for war," he explained.

He added that his conscience was keeping him from recommending that the congregants get guns too. His conscience and perhaps the fact that lacking a business like kidnapping to fund a military-style arsenal, most congregation members could never match the gangs' firepower, which surpassed even that of the Haitian National Police. In areas ruled by young men armed for war, the Sermon on the Mount was being interpreted differently. "Blessed are the meek: for they shall inherit the earth" no longer applied.

"The way we're living in this country right now, the only earth the meek will inherit is the cemetery," my artist friend concurred.

On July 14, 2022, Haitian customs officials confiscated seventeen semiautomatic weapons, twelve shotguns, and four pistols from containers arriving from Miami and addressed to Haiti's Episcopal Church, exposing a weapons smuggling ring that led to three church officials being charged for arms trafficking and money laundering. A few months later, Haitians in different areas organized self-defense groups in a zero-tolerance swift-justice movement called Bwa Kale, or peeled wood. Like *mawozo*, the term *bwa kale* has several figurative meanings, including an erection, or, as Jon Lee Anderson wrote in the *New Yorker* in July 2023, "a Shaft up the Ass."

The best-known incident of Bwa Kale happened in Port-au-Prince in April 2023 when police intercepted a minibus carrying fourteen pistol-toting gang members. A crowd gathered at the scene and pressured the police to turn the men over, after which the crowd stoned them to death and then burned their bodies, just as the gangs had, for years, killed their neighbors and incinerated their corpses. Later, the gangs would return in full force in an operation they called *zam pale* (weapons speak), expanding their territory through even more brutal massacres, including one in which they mowed down dozens of church members as they marched toward gang-occupied neighborhoods carrying sticks and machetes.

On October 31, 2021, it was reported on Haitian media that Patrice Michel Dérénoncourt, a well-known attorney, criminologist, engineer, and academic who was kidnapped the same day as the missionaries, was killed by his kidnappers because his family couldn't produce the $900,000 ransom they had requested. Nine years earlier, on August 27, 2012, Dérénoncourt had posted what looked like a passport picture on his Facebook page, and a friend of his had jokingly reacted, writing, "Ou vin jèn anpil wi lol! Ou sanble w fenk milyonè." (You're looking very youthful. LOL. You look like you just became a millionaire.) To which Dérénoncourt had good-humoredly replied, "Gen lè ou anvi fè yo kidnape m." (Seems like you're trying to get me kidnapped.) Kidnapping was common enough in Port-au-Prince to inspire jokes like this whenever having money or coming into money was discussed publicly, even among Haitians outside the country who were considering visiting.

Soon after his death was announced, I watched an old interview with Dérénoncourt on a Haiti-based book program, which was recorded at a Radio Television Caraïbes studio in Port-au-Prince. The program's moniker, *Des livres et vous* (Books and You), is a pun on *delivrez vous* (deliver yourself), for which the show's well-read and enthusiastic host, Dangelo Néard, who at the time was head of Haiti's National Library, makes a passionate case in the opening montage by declaring: "If people write, it's because the world is an act of language. Language is a tool of significance, deliverance."

On the December 13, 2019, episode featuring Dérénoncourt, both men sat on chairs that looked like they'd been carved out of bookshelves. Néard was wearing a ginger-colored jacket over one of his signature colorful shirts, this one adorned with butterflies. Dérénoncourt was wearing a mauve plaid shirt, dark pants, a beige jacket, and a matching ivy cap. Dérénoncourt, a voracious reader, was asked by Néard how he'd developed his love of reading. Dérénoncourt said that his father was a university professor and his mother a school principal and French teacher. When Dérénoncourt was a teenager, his father made him read the Bible as punishment, demanding that he write summaries of, memorize, and recite passages that taught specific lessons related to his offense. Dérénoncourt spent time with many prominent Haitian intellectuals, including his father's good friend, the writer and painter Frankétienne. He also spent hours discussing books and other subjects with his father's university students when they stopped by his house.

"I grew up in an environment where books were adored, where books represented the ultimate quest for knowledge," Dérénoncourt said, eyeglasses in hand. "I fell into books. . . . My magic potion is books."

Dérénoncourt had inherited a family library containing hundreds of volumes, some over a century old. Néard asked him to introduce the audience to five he'd take with him to a desert island. Dérénoncourt immediately modified the assignment and said that he'd brought books he believed spoke in some way to the country's current reality. He hoped that the books he'd chosen would lead to a better understanding of the present and "a partial improvement of the future."

The first book he introduced was Makenzy Orcel's *Les immortelles* (*The Immortals*), translated into English by Nathan Dize. The thirty-six-year-old Orcel's first novel describes a collabora-

tion between a writer and an unnamed sex worker who wants the
writer to tell the story of her colleague Shakira, who died during
the January 12, 2010, earthquake.

"Let's begin. I'll talk. You, the writer, you write. You transform," the sex worker tells the writer. Dérénoncourt had chosen this book, he said, because understanding others, including
our most maligned neighbors, "allows us to evolve, to be more
human." His second choice was Friedrich Nietzsche's hybrid phi-
losophy and experimental fiction work *Thus Spoke Zarathustra*.
Dérénoncourt was particularly fond of this often-quoted line: "In
truth, man is a polluted river. One must be a sea, to receive a polluted river and not be defiled."

His third choice was "Autre lamentation" (Another Lament),
a poem from *Le fou d'Elsa*, by Louis Aragon, a French poet and
cofounder of the surrealist movement.

> Ô sable divisé dans les mains souveraines
> Cruel à toi-même à toi-même confronté
> Peuple qui n'es que sang qu'on verse en vérité
> Qu'entrailles de chevaux sur l'arène qu'on traîne
>
> Regarde celui-là ton pareil et qu'on tue
> Ils t'ont donné la pierre et le couteau pour être
> Le bourreau de toi-même à te choisir un maître
> Et les coups de ton bras sur qui les portes-tu

My attempt at a partial translation:

> *O divided sand in sovereign hands*
> *Cruel to yourself and against yourself pitted*
> *A nation whose blood keeps being spilled*
> *Like horse entrails across showground lands*

Look at those like you whom they are killing
They gave you the stone and the knife to be
Your own executioner. On your master agree.
And with your blows, whom are you striking?

When he was asked why he chose that particular poem by Aragon, Dérénoncourt answered: "Haiti today. The pain, the violence, the tearing apart of brothers, the tearing apart of a nation."

"Do you think Haiti today is 'divided sand'?" Néard asked him.

"I don't even have to say it," he replied. "Everyone can see it. This division, this tearing apart, is palpable, visible. It now surpasses politics. We are at a point of rupture."

His fourth selection was *Ultravocal*, the genre-bending first novel by the eighty-five-year-old Frankétienne, one of the founders of Spiralism, a literary movement Frankétienne started in the 1960s, during the Duvalier dictatorship, with the writers Jean-Claude Fignolé and René Philoctète. Spiralism, according to Paulin, the novelist character of Frankétienne's 1968 novel *Mûr à crever* (translated by Kaiama L. Glover as *Ready to Burst*), "uses the Complete Genre, in which novelistic description, poetic breath, theatrical effect, narratives, stories, autobiographical sketches, and fiction all coexist harmoniously."

Dérénoncourt's fifth book merited an explanation from Néard, who said that in his four years of hosting the show, no one had ever chosen a book cowritten by Lorimer Denis, a Haitian ethnologist and cofounder of Haiti's Black nationalist *noirisme* movement, and the former dictator François "Papa Doc" Duvalier. The book was *Extraits des oeuvres ethnographiques du François Duvalier et Lorimer Denis* (Extracts from the Ethnographic Works of François Duvalier and Lorimer Denis). Duvalier was a medical doctor and a former public health minister who helped eradicate the bacterial infection yaws in rural Haiti before becoming president in 1957. Soon after Duvalier was sworn into office, he declared himself president for life, created a militia (the Tonton Macoutes) that committed untold atrocities in his name, and imprisoned, exiled, or executed his detractors and political opponents. François Duvalier remained in power until he died in 1971, when his son, Jean-Claude "Baby Doc," replaced him, carrying on with the regime until he left for France after massive protests and international pressure in 1986. "Is this a provocation?" Néard asked Dérénoncourt. "Why are François Duvalier and Lorimer Denis on my show?"

Because part of Duvalier's original message has remained relevant, Dérénoncourt explained while leafing through a copy of the very large book on his lap. He was not being revisionist or excusing the dictatorship, he said. He thought it was worth pointing out that Duvalier, in his academic work with Lorimer, reminded Haitians not to abandon the country's rural class. To grow his urban base during his fourteen years as president for life, Duvalier aggravated rural misery by busing thousands of rural residents to the capital, forcing them to trade off their ancestral plots of land for life in Port-au-Prince shantytowns, competing for jobs in American factories, where they made baseballs or T-shirts for less than a dollar a day. Later his son, Jean-Claude, contracted out both the rural and urban poor to work as sugarcane workers in the Dominican Republic, where some of their descendants are still denied citizenship decades later.

"We must go to the roots of these problems because these problems are not simply material. They are also mental," Dérénoncourt added regarding the Lorimer/Duvalier book.

On May 31, 2021, on another program on the same station, *L'Invité du midi* (Noon-Hour Guest), Dérénoncourt said that a genuine national dialogue in Haiti shouldn't involve only politicians and political parties but should also take place between people from different social classes, particularly between the haves and the have-nots.

"How can we get along?" he said, throwing out some possible questions that might be raised. "It's fine that you earn money, but what about the others? What will you give them? What's the limit to the amount of profit I can make? That's the national dialogue, which should happen even before the dialogue between the politicians. The politicians are just passing through, and sometimes they come up with good ideas. Sometimes they come up with wacky ideas when the reality is hunger. The reality is work. The reality is education. To raise the country's educational level, the rich must come to some agreement with the poor. The rich must agree to earn less and pay taxes. The number of people who can become rich must grow. Contributing to the country's social evolution is the rich's best protection."

The host, Samy Janvier, then asked him whether the country might be headed for civil war.

"I don't know. That's not my specialty," he said, looking uneasy. "But everyone has their knives out, both those in power and those in the opposition."

"How do we get out of all this?" Janvier pleaded.

The people need leaders who can create a framework and structure for the state, he said. "Only those who dream of better can do better. We must sit together and talk. If constant fighting benefits the politicians, it does not benefit the people. The people don't need politicians as much as leaders who can guide them toward their dreams."

At the end of their conversation, after he was thanked by Samy Janvier, Patrice Michel Dérénoncourt said, "If I was useful, that's good. If I shocked people, I'm sorry."

As the missionaries entered their fourth week in captivity, Christian Aid Ministries posted daily updates on their website. The updates often began with a mention of the number of days the missionaries had been in captivity, followed by a Bible verse or some message of support they had received.

Prayers were offered for the kidnappers in this November 10 update: "The kidnapping took place on October 16, and we are still waiting and praying for the group of 17 to be released if God so wills. We request continued prayer for the kidnappers, that God would soften their hearts and that they would experience His love and goodness. As you pray, remember the millions of Haitians who are suffering through a time of serious upheaval and unrest. We desire that God would be their 'refuge and strength, a very present help in trouble' Psalm 46:1."

As the missionaries entered their fifth week in captivity, two were released.

That day the Christian Aid Ministries update read, in part: "We have learned that two of the hostages in Haiti were released. . . . While we rejoice at this release, our hearts are with the fifteen people who are still being held. Continue to lift up the remaining hostages before the Lord."

Three more missionaries were released a few weeks later; then as they neared the two-month anniversary of their captivity, the remaining twelve were said to have escaped. By their telling, they left while the gang members were asleep. They braved the mountainous terrain of Croix-des-Bouquets by moonlight with a baby and toddler in tow until they were found by Good Samaritans who led them to safety. Few in Haiti and the global Haitian diaspora believed that they had escaped, the more logical interpretation being that 400 Mawozo simply allowed them to walk away after receiving a ransom. The missionaries got a testimony, and the gang got to appear even more powerful, their own kind of testimony.

This was not the first time epic events had occurred in Croix-des-Bouquets. In 1770, after its first location sank beneath the sea during a massive earthquake that reverberated as far as Jamaica, the town was moved to its current location—founded by Spanish royal decree in 1749, on land donated by those who had stolen it from the indigenous population and whose names still remain on Bellanton, Santo, Savane d'Oublon, and Noailles. Legend has it that Croix-des-Bouquets was named after a tradition in which passing Spaniards placed bouquets of flowers at the foot of a large cross they had planted at the town's entrance. That it was home-grown crosses, Liautaud's, that awed others and brought metal *dekoupe* to the center of life in Croix-des-Bouquets, as well as to the world's attention, shows that Haitian artists are most definitely wozo.

Writing the Self and Others

In the summer of 2018, while I was in Haiti, my uncle Frank, my father's youngest brother, wandered out of his house early one morning, half-dressed and disoriented. A neighbor spotted him and alerted my cousin Mendy, his daughter. My uncle was experiencing some signs of dementia. Suddenly, or perhaps not so suddenly, my uncle's past had vanished. An entire segment of our family history, of which he was the sole caretaker, was no longer available to us. Or to himself.

Families, as my suddenly silenced uncle used to say, expand like ripples in a pond. Migration forces you to remake your family, as well as yourself. Family is not only made up of your living relatives. It is elders long buried and generations yet unborn, with stories as bridges and potential portals. Family is whoever is left when everyone else is gone. It is whoever is cleaning up at the end of the party or the funeral repast. It is that person whose one nod might comfort you more than hundreds of words from someone else. Family members help you carry your dreams and memories.

When I first heard about my uncle's illness—this was one among many others—I wondered whether he could still dream, and if so what those dreams were about. His own dead parents and siblings? My grandparents and aunts and uncle, my father? His childhood home in the mountains of southern Haiti? His four decades spent as a factory worker, cabdriver, and car-service owner in Brooklyn, New York? His five sons and daughters? The final years he'd imagined as a proud grandfather embraced by a large brood of grandchildren, possibly even great-grandchildren?

I wondered if his dreams were vivid, like movies of his own making. Did he also hallucinate and have night terrors? Like a lot of dementia patients, he could have been suffering from sundowning—evening agitation and restlessness. Could he also have been struggling with sunrising, when after a night of unease, in the morning he would barely recognize what's real and what's a dream? Perhaps this was what drove him into the street, at dawn. Thinking of "sundowning" and "sunrising" made me imagine him as Phaethon, dragging the sun behind him across the sky. Was it possible that my uncle could no longer recall his early struggling days in the United States, remember his fear of snow, or his many slips and falls on black ice as he was heading to work at a garment factory during the day, and to drive his taxicab at night? Might he have forgotten the births of his children, or the death of his wife?

Family legacies, my uncle and father used to say, are not only about traditions and values passed on from generation to generation. They are also about the actions we take or choose not to take. In the mountain village where my uncle and father were born, a single deed could mark, or stain, your family's reputation for generations, placing you in a hierarchy that, even if it was enforced only by gossip or shame, might still decide the fate of your progeny. I am not sure that's still true, but my father held on to that notion until his death, in part because it was taught to him by his father, who had learned it from his father. This is why he and my uncle had to leave the ancestral village and move to the capital, my uncle would say. Though neither he nor his siblings had committed shameful acts, they longed to start over in a new place where the generational burden was less weighty. Their new beginning was meant to be a reboot, though, not an erasure.

I was seventeen when my uncle's wife suddenly died after prematurely giving birth to their youngest daughter, Emmanuella, six months into her pregnancy. Though he was heartbroken, my uncle also looked relieved that out of that terrible tragedy had emerged a three-pound, six-ounce beautiful little girl.

Weeks later, when he was finally allowed to bring his daughter home, my parents and I went to visit them. My cousin Emmanuella was curled up in her crib, sucking her index and middle fingers intently as though she were nursing. My parents and I looked down at her in amazement. My cousin looked so fragile that we were afraid to pick her up.

"Li pa p kase nan men w," my uncle told me, as if reading my thoughts. She will not break in your hands.

In whose hands will she break then? I remembered thinking, but did not say.

"Li gen la vi nan li," my uncle added. She has life in her. Then in his heavily accented English, emphatically added, "She has traveled a long way to be here. She has fought a lot to be here. This is your family."

I picked up my baby cousin and pulled her close to my chest. Her eyes kept fluttering as she continued to suckle her fingers. She had been at that intangible crossroads where she entered this world as her mother abruptly exited. My uncle was right. She had plenty of life in her. There was plenty of spirit in her too.

The Aztec considered women who die during childbirth to be

fallen warriors. These women are also thought to travel with the sun throughout the latter part of the day, settling in at sundown. My cousin's life began with a battle, which her mother is not around to recount, and which her father no longer remembers.

Newborns are the most obvious signs that families are growing. Births thrust us into the future and replace what the deaths take away. Now when children are born into my family, I don't necessarily get to hold them right away. They are often born in different states and different countries, far away from where I live. Sometimes I first meet them in person when they are already walking and talking, even though I first see them online, or attached to texts and WhatsApp messages, soon after they are born. They are still my family, light-filled faces on phones though they be, beyond the reach of touch though they be. One day I too might struggle to remember their names and faces.

I was with my uncle Frank when he died in March 2022. I flew from Miami to New York to visit him. He had been bedridden, and primarily unconscious for some time. When I walked into the hospital room, my cousin Mendy was singing him a Haitian gospel song he loved. I leaned over and, with my lips close to his ear, whispered, "Uncle, this is Nounoune [my family nickname]. I came to see you."

Tears rolled down his face, piercing through his half-closed eyes.

I reached for his hands, his fists long balled by arthritis, and held them the way he'd held mine so many times when I was a girl. Mendy, who had been with him nearly every day for almost a decade of illnesses, offered to grab me a chair from the hallway. I accepted. When Mendy stepped out of the room, my uncle's chest rose and fell, and he stopped breathing.

Though his ending felt abrupt, something about it was not. He was the last of his generation still alive. His death was both a beginning and an end, just like Emmanuella's birth had been. At fifty-three, I had been thrust into becoming one of the oldest people on my father's side of the family; it had turned me into an elder.

My uncle once asked me why I never wrote about him.

"Consider yourself lucky," I said. "I don't write happy things."

"Then write about me when I die," he said.

I also write, I want to tell those young writers I once visited in Fond-des-Blancs, to keep my promises to the dead.

During the summer of 2020, my daughter Mira took a writing class online. Taught by the writer Erica N. Cardwell, the class was called "Writing the Self."

Mira and I were both won over by the course description:

> *Imagine: "The Essay" is a body of water—far-flung and teeming into the distance. And you, the writer, are alone on shore. Will you enter the water? And if so, how will you swim? Or will you stand on shore as the water splashes against your ankles?*

"I wish I could take this class," I told Mira.

What I meant was that I wished I could have taken this class when I was fifteen. I have read most of the assigned essays and revisited some, which I read out aloud to Mira. We read "When We Dead Awaken: Writing as Re-Vision," by the poet Adrienne Rich, where she told us that "writing is re-naming." We then read Audre Lorde's "Poetry Is Not a Luxury" (1977), where Lorde reminds us, "There are no new pains. We have felt them all already."

In an August 30, 1979, interview between the two women,

Lorde cites her choral poem "Need: A Chorale for Black Woman Voices," which is about the frequent silence around the lives and deaths of murdered Black women and girls:

> *How much of this truth can I bear?*
> *to see*
> *and still live*
> *unblinded?*
> *How much of this pain can I use?*

Every time Mira finds herself in a new situation, I remember, among other things, when she was eleven years old and we arrived at a friend's birthday party, where she tried to sit next to another girl. The girl turned to her and shouted very loudly "No!" Looking heartbroken, Mira limped over to where I was standing. My reaction in that moment was cowardly. I put my arms around her and asked if she wanted to go home. Thankfully, she wanted to stay. Eventually Mira found some other friends and enjoyed herself. At the end of the party, the birthday girl's parents lit some sky lanterns that were supposed to float down the bay behind their home and glide away from the shore, toward the sunset. Thick gloomy clouds blocked the sunset, and most of the lanterns turned to ash, on the ground. Had we left the party, Mira might have missed out on an opportunity to discover, or rediscover, that things sometimes go differently than planned or hoped for, and though home can be a safe place, we shouldn't always rush back there.

When I asked Mira what she was writing for Cardwell's class, she demurred, then told me that her first piece would be about a tree she and her friends used to love to sit under during recess in elementary school. It was their safe place, their sanctuary.

"The same tree where a boy hit you in the forehead with a rock?" I asked.

Why did I think she'd want to write about the worst thing that has ever happened to her under that tree? she asked.

Because that's what I would do.

"I'm not going to write about that," she said.

She wrote about digging for worms under that tree with her girlfriends, most of whom ended up going to different schools and having different friends and were no longer in touch with her.

Once while I was driving her home from that same school, we were listening to an audio version of Tillie Olsen's "I Stand Here Ironing," a short story about a mother discussing her troubled teenage daughter on the phone. I can never revisit that story without thinking of my mother and all the ironing she did in her bedroom on Sunday nights, first in our crowded two-room apartment in Port-au-Prince, and later in the two-bedroom apartment my parents rented in East Flatbush, and the house they later bought in that same part of Brooklyn. When Olsen's character speaks of having to send her daughter away, first to family members, then to a girls' group home, and of the daughter's ensuing separation anxiety, I always feel a lump in my throat. In the car with Mira that day was the first time I was hearing that story as a mother, and in the presence of one of my two daughters.

At the end of the story, I turned to look at Mira in the back seat, and tears were streaming down her face. Overeager and excited, and still being a writer, I asked her what exactly about the story was making her cry. Which part moved her? Was it the daughter not being able to keep her mother's letters, or any other personal possessions, with her in the group home? Or was it the final line of the story where the mother wants her daughter to know that the daughter is "more than this dress on the ironing-board, helpless before the iron"?

After I pushed a bit too much, Mira answered, "I think I cried because you were crying."

Years after my mother died, I kept finding some of her belongings around my house. Midway through the essay class, while going through a box of old things, I found a wooden machete, a memento my mother bought while she was on a Caribbean cruise. I also found a small book my mother had owned since it was first published by Watch Tower Bible and Tract Society in 1979, *Comment s'assurer une vie de famille heureuse.* The original English title was *Making Your Family Life Happy Forever.* The text was illustrated with watercolor-like images, including many happy couples and families. The book was one of many Jehovah's Witnesses tracts given to my mother by her sisters, who'd remained Witnesses after my mother became a Pentecostal like my father. The book was padded with thirteen old black-and-white postcard-sized pictures I had never seen before. Based on the time stamps and notes written on the back of the pictures, I figured out that these youthful-looking, elegantly dressed young men and women posing in front of drapes inside professional photo studios were friends from my parents' youth in Haiti; some they had known separately, and others they came to know together after they were married. Like my parents, many of them were probably long dead.

On the front and back pages of this book are the phone numbers of other friends that my mother had jotted down at different times over a number of years. The key to a happy family life was Jehovah. I did not have to read the book to be made aware of its intended message. Still I did, and in reading it I found that the only part of the book that was both underlined and highlighted was a reference to the story of Rachel and Jacob. Rachel, a shepherdess, finally married her cousin Jacob after he spent seven years working for her father to gain her hand. Like me, my mother was a sucker for stories of people kept apart by circumstances beyond their control. On that same page was the only piece of marginalia in the entire book, the words *rang social* (social status?), written in my mother's tiny scrawl.

My mother never wanted me to write about her. It made her feel unshielded, exposed. I now understand that protective impulse, something akin to fearing the loss of your soul to the lens of a camera. The older I get and the fewer places there are to disappear in this all-seeing and all-knowing world, the more I want to hide, though Lorde has warned that what is most important "must be spoken, made verbal and shared, even at the risk of having it bruised or misunderstood." At times, fiction remains my only veil. When I write, I told those young writers in Fond-des-Blancs, I sometimes break promises both to myself and to others, to the living and the dead.

As she neared the end of the essay class, I told Mira I wanted to write about my mother's wooden machete. (I hadn't yet figured out how to write about the Jehovah's Witnesses book and the pictures.) The machete also seemed like a much more apparent symbol. Instead I started writing about the time when Mira was six years old and we took my mother to the airport so she could return to her home in Brooklyn after a monthlong visit with us in Miami. Taking my mother to the airport and watching her leave always reminded me of my first concrete childhood memory, of being peeled off my mother's body on the day she left Haiti for the United States when I was four years old.

That day, at the airport in Miami, as Mira and I watched my mother merge into the crowd heading toward her gate, Mira screamed, "Manman!" at the top of her voice. My daughters usually called my mother Grann. Manman is what my brothers and

I called my mother, so hearing Mira call my mother Manman startled both me and my mother.

My mother turned around and stared at us. She seemed relieved that there was nothing physically wrong with either Mira or me. As other travelers dashed around her, my mother took a few steps in our direction, then stopped. She looked like she wanted to walk back to us, but knew she could not. Returning to us would just require another goodbye. Her life, at that time, was in New York, as were her house, her friends, and her church. Her flight was already boarding. She slowly raised the hand that had been resting on her carry-on bag and waved once more, then she turned around and continued walking to her gate.

I asked Mira if she remembered that day. She remembered us taking my mother to the airport a bunch of times, she said, but did not remember ever calling after her. But she did recall another moment at the same place.

Once, while my husband and daughters and I were waiting to board a flight to New York with my mother, my mother went to look for a restroom and accidently walked past security, leaving the boarding area without her boarding pass or her cell phone. When our plane began boarding, Mira and I went looking for her and found her pleading, in her hesitant English, with an impatient TSA officer to let her back in, or at least to accompany her to the gate, and to us.

"She looked so lost and so scared," Mira remembered. "Like she thought she'd never see us again."

That day, I had also feared that we might never see my mother again, that she might end up on the wrong flight to some distant country, or as an eternal ghost in the airport, passing everyone by, or that, strangely, she might turn into a little girl who is left behind, by me. That moment also made me realize why travel, particularly air travel, is sometimes nerve-racking for me, why I stay up the night before putting my life in order, cleaning my house from top to bottom, and reminding my loved ones where important documents are kept. I do not want to leave anyone behind, but I know the choice will not always be mine, just as it was not entirely my mother's.

The words my mother would later use to recount to her friends the experience of being lost in the airport trickle back into my mind on the last day of the essay class.

M te pèdi. Yo jwen mwen.

Vwayaj la te kontinye.

I was lost. They found me.

The journey continued.

I too have been lost, but eventually, words, stories, find me. Once again, I have entered this body of water. I am no longer alone on the shore. *Vwayaj la a p kontinye.* Our journey continues.

APPENDIX

Plage
Roland Chassagne

Nuit. Bercement mélancolique
Des palmes.
Tu chantes. Ta voix fragile
S'évanouit loin,—
Sur les plages du silence.

Nuit. Le vent est d'une lourdeur
fraîche. Derrière moi,
J'ai refoulé toutes mes rancoeurs
Et tu sais que ma vie est une allée
Solitaire que, seule, tu longes.

Nuit. Nuit divine et triste. Là-haut
la lune nomade voyage dans les brumes.
Et plus ne reviendra la nuit triste,
Je le sens..

Laisse-moi prendre tes mains
Et te dire des choses simples
Et inoubliables . .

Parce que nous étions seuls,
Près du rivage, sous ce dais
de palmes, et qu'on s'aimait,
Le bonheur était intense et
Inexprimable.

Shore

Night

The sad cradling
Of palms.
You sing. Your frail voice
Faints afar—
Where the sands of silence are.

Night

Heavy, heavy the wind
But sweet! I have buried
My hatreds deep.
My life is a lone pathway
Which only you can keep.

Night

Night—divine and sad.
A nomad moon wanders away . . .
Never more will be a night so sad.
Never, never, can be . . . .

Your hands—give them to me,
Let me speak, and simply
Words you can not forget.

Night

We're alone—
And the sea . . . .
And the cradling palms are thick.

Translated into English by Edna Worthley Underwood

Bibliography

Abi-Habib, Maria, "Haiti's Leader Kept a List of Drug Traffickers. His Assassins Came for It," *New York Times*, December 12, 2021, https://www.nytimes.com/2021/12/12/world/americas/jovenel -moise-haiti-president-drug-traffickers.html.

Abi-Habib, Maria, and Constant Méheut, "Morally, They Are Lost: Gangs in Haiti, Breaking a Taboo, Target the Church," *New York Times*, October 22, 2021, https://www.nytimes.com/2021/10/22 /world/americas/haiti-gangs-church.html. .

Abi-Habib, Maria, Natalie Kitroeff, Frances Robles, and Nick Madigan, "US Arrests Four More in the Assassination of Haiti's President," *New York Times*, February 14, 2023, https://www .nytimes.com/2023/02/14/world/americas/haiti-president -assassination-americans.html.

Al Jazeera, "Man Pleads Guilty in US Probe of Haiti President Assassination," March 24, 2023, https://www.aljazeera.com/news /2023/3/24/man-pleads-guilty-in-us-probe-of-haiti-president -assassination.

Anderson, Jon Lee, "Haiti Held Hostage," *New Yorker*, July 17, 2023, https://www.newyorker.com/magazine/2023/07/24/haiti-held -hostage.

Aragon, Louis, *Le fou d'Elsa*, Gallimard, 1963.

Baldwin, James, *Another Country*, Vintage, 1992.

Baldwin, James, *Go Tell It on the Mountain*, Everyman's Library, 2016.

Baldwin, James, *James Baldwin, The Last Interview and Other Conversations*, Melville House, 2014.

Baldwin, James, *The Devil Finds Work*, Vintage International, 2011.

Baldwin, James, *The Fire Next Time*, Vintage, 1992.

Beattie, Ann, "The Distillation of Lavender: Jayne Hinds Bidaut's Photographs," in *More to Say: Essays and Appreciations*, Nonpareil Books, 2023.

Berger, Miriam, "Who Is 400 Mawozo, the Haitian Gang Accused of Kidnapping American Missionaries?" *Washington Post*, October 17, 2021.

Best, Wallace, "The Fear of Black Bodies in Motion," *Huffington Post*, February 3, 2015, https://www.huffpost.com/entry/the-fear-of-black-bodies-in-motion_b_6268672.

Boumediene, Lakhdar, "I Was Force-Fed at Guantanamo. What Guards Are Doing Now Is Worse," *New Republic*, October 30, 2017, https://newrepublic.com/article/145549/force-fed-guantanamo-guards-now-worse.

Byatt, A. S., *Possession*, Vintage, 1991.

Charles, Jacqueline, "Legalization of Abortion, Gay Rights Has Haiti Churches Up In Arms, Criticizing President," *Miami Herald*, August 6, 2020.

Charles, Jacqueline, "They Were Live on Facebook When an Armed Man Stormed In and Kidnapped Them in Haiti," *Miami Herald*, April 2, 2021, https://www.heraldmailmedia.com/story/news/2021/04/03/they-were-live-on-facebook-when-an-armed-man-stormed-in-and-kidnapped-them-in-haiti/43740399/.

Charles, Jacqueline, "Two Years after Haiti President's Death, the Mystery Yields More Questions than Answers," *Miami Herald*, July 7, 2023, https://www.miamiherald.com/news/nation-world/world/americas/haiti/article277068068.html.

Charles, Jacqueline, and Jay Weaver, "Grenade-dropping Drones, a

Paranoid President, Guards Who Ran: Latest on Haiti Assassination," *Miami Herald*, September 20, 2021.

Charles, Jacqueline, and Jay Weaver, "Haiti Judge Concludes Inquiry into Presidential Assassination, Points Finger at Widow," *Miami Herald*, February 19, 2024, https://www.miamiherald.com/news/nation-world/world/americas/haiti/article285645817.html.

Ciechalski, Suzanne, and Caroline Radnofsky, "Christian Charity Says Its Manager Knew for Years One of Their Missionaries Admitted to Abusing Children," NBC News, October 6, 2019, https://www.nbcnews.com/news/us-news/christian-charity-paid-alleged-sex-abuse-victims-former-haiti-missionary-n1049916.

Clawson, Victoria, Elizabeth Detweiler, and Laura Ho, "Litigating as Law Students: An Inside Look at Haitian Centers Council," *Yale Law Journal*, June 1994, https://www.jstor.org/stable/797050.

Collins, Merle, *Because the Dawn Breaks!: Poems Dedicated to the Grenadian People*, Karia Press, 1985.

Coto, Dánica, "Haiti Priest Recounts Abduction by Gang Holding Missionaries," Associated Press, November 9, 2021.

Coto, Dánica, and Alberto Arce, "Desperate Haitians Suffocate under Growing Power of Gangs," Pulitzer Center, October 22, 2021, https://pulitzercenter.org/stories/desperate-haitians-suffocate-under-growing-power-gangs.

Danticat, Edwidge, *Breath, Eyes, Memory*, Soho Press, 1994.

Danticat, Edwidge, *Krik? Krak!*, Soho Press, 1995.

Depestre, René, *Journal d'un animal marin*, Editions Pierre Seghers, 1965.

Depestre, René, *A Rainbow for the Christian West*, translated with an introduction by Joan Dayan (Colin Dayan), University of Massachusetts Press, 1977.

Depestre, René, *Un arc-en-ciel pour l'Occident Chrétien*, Editions Présence Africaine, 1957.

Dias, Elizabeth, "Haiti Missionaries Describe Dramatic Escape from Kidnappers," *New York Times*, December 20, 2021, https://www.nytimes.com/2021/12/20/us/haiti-missionaries-escape.html.

Duvalier, François, Lorimer Denis, and Marcelin Jocelyn, *Extraits des oeuvres ethnographiques du docteur François Duvalier et Lorimer Denis* (*Extracts from the Ethnographic Works of François Duvalier and Lorimer Denis*), Imprimerie de L'État, Port-au-Prince, 1962.

Evans, Mari, *Black Women Writers (1950–1980): A Critical Evaluation*, Anchor, 1984.

Fournier, Arthur M., with Daniel Herlihy, *Zombie Curse: A Doctor's 25-year Journey into the Heart of the AIDS Epidemic in Haiti*, Joseph Henry Press, 2006.

Frankétienne, *Ready to Burst*, translated by Kaiama L. Glover, Archipelago, 2014.

Frankétienne, *Ultravocal*, Dimensions, 2005.

García Márquez, Gabriel, *Chronicle of a Death Foretold*, Vintage, 1982.

García Márquez, Gabriel, *Collected Stories*, Harper Perennial Modern Classics, 2008.

García Márquez, Gabriel, *Love in the Time of Cholera*, Vintage, 2007.

García Márquez, Gabriel, *One Hundred Years of Solitude*, Harper Perennial Modern Classics, 2006.

Haiti Libre, "The First Baptist Church of Port-au-Prince Victim of Heavily Armed Men," September 27, 2021, https://www.haitilibre .com/en/news-34844-haiti-flash-the-first-baptist-church-of -port-au-prince-victim-of-heavily-armed-men.html.

Hansberry, Lorraine, *A Raisin in the Sun*, Vintage, 2004.

Hurston, Zora Neale, *Dust Tracks on a Road: An Autobiography*, Harper Perennial Modern Classics, 2006.

Hurston, Zora Neale, *Tell My Horse: Voodoo and Life in Haiti and Jamaica*, Harper and Row, 1938.

Hurston, Zora Neale, *Their Eyes Were Watching God*, Amistad, 2006.

Johnson, Jake, "Head of Haiti's Palace Guard Subject of US Law Enforcement Investigation into Arms Trafficking," Center for Economic and Policy Research, July 9, 2021, https://cepr.net /exclusive-head-of-haitis-palace-guard-subject-of-us-law -enforcement-investigation-into-arms-trafficking/.

Joseph, Murdith, "Weapons, Ammunition, Fake Cash Found in

Episcopal Church of Haiti Containers," *Haitian Times*, July 16, 2022, https://haitiantimes.com/2022/07/16/weapons-ammunition-fake-cash-found-in-episcopal-church-of-haiti-containers/.

Kincaid, Jamaica, *The Autobiography of My Mother*, FSG Classics, 2013.

Kruis, Pat, "Madras Missionary, Held Hostage in Haiti, Tells His Story," *Portland Tribune*, January 5, 2022, https://www.koin.com/news/madras-missionary-held-hostage-in-haiti-tells-his-story/.

Lester, Julius, "James Baldwin—Reflections of a Maverick," *New York Times*, May 27, 1984.

London, Jack, *The Call of the Wild*, Modern Library Classics, 1998.

Lorde, Audre, *Chosen Poems, Old and New*, Norton, 1982.

Lorde, Audre, *Sister Outsider*, Crossing Press Feminist Series, 2013.

Marshall, Paule, "From the Poets in the Kitchen," *New York Times*, January 9, 1989.

Marshall, Paule, *Triangular Road*, Civitas Books, 2009.

Matei, Adrienne, "Plastic Is Already in Blood, Breast Milk, and Placentas. Now It May Be in Our Brains," *The Guardian*, May 1, 2023, https://www.theguardian.com/commentisfree/2023/may/01/plastic-is-already-in-blood-breast-milk-and-placentas-now-it-may-be-in-our-brains.

Monet, Aja, *My Mother Was a Freedom Fighter*, Haymarket Books, 2017.

Morrison, Toni, "A Bench by the Road," *UU World*, January-February 1989, https://www.uuworld.org/articles/a-bench-by-road.

Morrison, Toni, *Beloved*, Vintage, 2004.

Morrison, Toni, *The Bluest Eye*, Vintage, 2007.

Morrison, Toni, *The Nobel Lecture in Literature, 1993*, Knopf, 1994.

Morrison, Toni, *Song of Solomon*, Random House, 1977.

Morrison, Toni, *Sula*, Random House, 1973.

Morrison, Toni, *Tar Baby*, Vintage, 2004.

Nietzsche, Friedrich, *Thus Spoke Zarathustra*, translated from the German by Thomas Common, Dover, 1999.

Olsen, Tillie, *Tell Me a Riddle, Requa I, and Other Works*, Bison Original, 2013.

Orcel, Makenzy, *The Immortals*, translated from the French by Nathan H. Dize, SUNY Press, 2020.

Porter, Catherine, Constant Méheut, Selam Gebrekidan, and Matt Apuzzo, "The Ransom" *New York Times*, May 23, 2022.

Price, Mark, "How Did Piles of Haiti's Trash End Up on NC Beaches? Hurricane Florence Is a Suspect," *Charlotte Observer*, September 25, 2018.

Rhys, Jean, *Wide Sargasso Sea*, Norton, 2016.

Rich, Adrienne, *Essential Essays: Culture, Politics, and the Art of Poetry*, Norton, 2019.

Rivers, Matt, "Haiti's First Lady Moïse Describes Husband's Assassination," *Anderson Cooper 360*, CNN, August 2, 2021, https://www.cnn.com/videos/world/2021/08/02/haiti-first-lady -rivers-intv-pkg-ac360-vpx.cnn.

Robles, Frances, "'They Thought I Was Dead': Haitian President's Widow Recounts Assassination," *New York Times*, July 30, 2021, https://www.nytimes.com/2021/07/30/world/americas/haiti -assassination-martine-moise-interview.html.

Shakespeare, William, *The Winter's Tale*, various editions.

Sharpe, Christina, *In the Wake: On Blackness and Being*, Duke University Press, 2016.

Thomas, Gessika, and Brian Ellsworth, "Haiti's 400 Mawozo Rose from Petty Crime Gang to Major Kidnapping Ring," Reuters, October 2, 2018.

Turtis, Richard Lee, "A World Destroyed, A Nation Imposed: The 1937 Haitian Massacre in the Dominican Republic," *Hispanic American Historical Review*, 2002.

Ulysse, Gina Athena, "Avant-Garde Rasanblaj (A Meditation on PÒTOPRENS): The Black Aesthetics of the first Black Republic," Pioneer Works, March 22, 2022, https://pioneerworks.org/broadcast /gina-athena-ulysse-potoprens.

Ulysse, Gina Athena, *Why Haiti Needs New Narratives: A Post-Quake Chronicle*, Wesleyan University Press, 2015.

Underwood, Edna Worthley, translator, *The Poets of Haiti: 1782–1934*, Mosher Press, 1934.

Ward, Jesmyn, ed., *The Fire This Time: A New Generation Speaks about Race*, Scribner, 2017.

Watch Tower Bible and Tract Society, *Comment s'assurer une vie de famille heureuse*, 1979.

Wilkerson, Isabel, *The Warmth of Other Suns: The Epic Story of America's Great Migration*, Vintage, 2011.

Wucker, Michele, *Why the Cocks Fight: Dominicans, Haitians, and the Struggle for Hispaniola*, Hill and Wang, 2000.

Zhang, Sarah, "Animals Are Migrating to the Great Pacific Garbage Patch," *Atlantic*, April 17, 2023.

Acknowledgments

I am deeply grateful to United States Artists and Sarah Arison for the 2020 United States Artists fellowship. I am also immensely grateful to Jan and Marica Vilcek and the Vilcek Foundation for the 2020 Vilcek Prize in Literature. Thank you Cherie Miot Abbanat and Ferry Cadet from Haiti Projects, and Erica N. Cardwell for the "Writing the Self" class in Barnard College's summer program. My deepest thanks to Rachel Arons and Brianna Milord, who have edited and fact-checked my pieces for the *New Yorker* online, as well as Veerly Huleatt and Caitrin Keiper at Plough. *Mèsi anpil* Regine Chassagne and Stanley Chassagne for our conversations about Roland Chassagne and much more. Thank you Ninaj Raoul, Guerline Joseph, Alix Cantave, and also to Jean-Jacques Solage and Tour Haiti.

Some of these pieces have been adapted from material previously published in *World Literature Today*, *Traffic East Magazine*, the *New Yorker*, *Stranger's Guide*, the *New York Times*, *Harper's Magazine*, *Plough*, the *New York Review of Books*, *O, the Oprah Magazine*, and *Aperture*. Thank you to Widline Cadet, whose work has deeply moved me and whose photograph *Seremoni Disparisyon #1 (Ritual [Dis]appearance #1)*, 2019, appears on the cover of this book.

EDWIDGE DANTICAT is the author of numerous books, most recently the story collection *Everything Inside*, winner of the Bocas Fiction Prize, the Story Prize, and the National Book Critics Circle Fiction Prize, and *The Art of Death*, a National Book Critics Circle finalist in Criticism. Her novels include *Breath, Eyes, Memory*, an Oprah Book Club selection, *Krik? Krak!*, a National Book Award finalist, and *The Farming of Bones*, an American Book Award winner. Her memoir, *Brother, I'm Dying*, was the winner of a National Book Critics Circle Award and a finalist for the National Book Award. Among other awards, she has received a MacArthur Fellowship, the Neustadt Prize, and the Vilcek Prize. She teaches at Columbia University.

Graywolf Press publishes risk-taking, visionary writers who transform culture through literature. As a nonprofit organization, Graywolf relies on the generous support of its donors to bring books like this one into the world.

This publication is made possible, in part, by the voters of Minnesota through a Minnesota State Arts Board Operating Support grant, thanks to a legislative appropriation from the arts and cultural heritage fund. Significant support has also been provided by other generous contributions from foundations, corporations, and individuals. To these supporters we offer our heartfelt thanks.

To learn more about Graywolf's books and authors
or make a tax-deductible donation, please visit
www.graywolfpress.org.

The text of *We're Alone* is set in Adobe Garamond Pro.
Book design by Rachel Holscher.
Composition by Bookmobile Design & Digital
Publisher Services, Minneapolis, Minnesota.
Manufactured by Friesens on acid-free,
100 percent postconsumer wastepaper.